What Others Are Saying

"Rusty has achieved the near ir ̣ write a book that educates, advc retaining a light-hearted playfu ̣ ....u to dogs. There is no more noble cau.. ̣an helping a dog, and it is my hope that this book will open more hearts to adopt their next canine companion."

Kim Gentry
Award winning singer/songwriter
Berteal

"It takes a brilliant writer to weave the profound words revealed in The Prayer of St. Francis into a book entitled Pee, Poop, Heartache and Love. Rusty Williams is that author. Williams' words are crafted in a manner that engages the reader ... and story after story had me asking really thought provoking questions about how I view life. A Winning Book."

Kevin Touhey
Bestselling author/motivational speaker
The Miracle of Optimism and *The Agony of Winning*

"As I read this book, I felt like I was there, going through the experience with them. I felt the love they were giving and receiving from the dogs. If you ever had a dog, had a friend with a dog, saw a dog – can spell the word dog – you need to read this book! I took away that whatever you give in life, you get back one hundred times over."

Michael Aronin
Comedian/Speaker/Actor
Lead role in Comedy Central's *Special Unit*

"In his chapters, as Rusty Williams muses on a dog's life and faithfully ponders St. Francis' prayer, he will help you laugh and cry and remember the importance of unconditional love. It's a fine, furry book that Williams has written!"

Larry Patten
Pastor/author
Companion For The Journey and *Another Companion For The Journey*

PEE, POOP, HEARTACHE,

AND

LOVE

PEE, POOP, HEARTACHE, AND LOVE

Life Lessons Learned From Fostering Shelter Dogs

RUSTY WILLIAMS

TATE PUBLISHING
AND ENTERPRISES, LLC

Published by Tate Publishing & Enterprises, LLC
127 E. Trade Center Terrace | Mustang, Oklahoma 73064 USA
1.888.361.9473 | www.tatepublishing.com

Tate Publishing is committed to excellence in the publishing industry. The company reflects the philosophy established by the founders, based on Psalm 68:11,
"The Lord gave the word and great was the company of those who published it."

Book design copyright © 2015 by Tate Publishing, LLC. All rights reserved.
Cover design by Nino Carlo Suico
Interior design by Jake Muelle

Published in the United States of America

ISBN: 978-1-68118-918-5
1. Pets / Dogs / General
2. Biography & Autobiography / General
15.07.16

Lord, make me an instrument of your peace.
Where there is hatred, let me sow love.
Where there is injury, pardon.
Where there is doubt, faith.
Where there is despair, hope.
Where there is darkness, light.
Where there is sadness, joy.

O Divine Master,
grant that I may not so much seek to be consoled, as to console;
to be understood, as to understand;
to be loved, as to love.
For it is in giving that we receive.
It is in pardoning that we are pardoned,
and it is in dying that we are born to Eternal Life.

Amen.

—The Prayer of Saint Francis

This book is dedicated to everyone involved with animal rescue organizations throughout the world and in memory of all the pets that are waiting for us on the other side of the Rainbow Bridge.

In honor of everyone fighting an orphan disease.

For Matt and Corey.

To Elissa.

Foreword

Some books are meant to be read by lots and lots of people. Rusty Williams' book is one of them. It's a book you'll immediately want to share with everyone you care about. Like a good movie, Pee, Poop, Heartache, and Love will make you laugh, and it will make you cry. And it will always keep you entertained. Most importantly, it will inspire you.

Now let me get one thing straight: This is a book about dogs and the amazing people who foster them. But it's more than that. Let me tell you why.

Each chapter comes with its own tale about a dog—and in some very funny instances, more than one dog—that Rusty and his wife Elissa care for until the foster care community can arrange an adoption. The stories are laugh out loud funny, suspenseful, and heartwarming. If you're a dog lover, or, I'll go even further—if you have ever cared for an animal—you're going to love this book. There are a lot of people already on my list who are going to get Pee, Poop, Heartache, and Love for the holidays.

But here's what I want to get right. Here's how this book is much more than just about foster dogs. Rusty is a truly wise man and a master storyteller, and like the great teachers through the ages, he weaves life lessons through his writing which will evoke your love, make you more grateful, give you more peace, and increase your joy. This book is ultimately about you.

Now, Rusty's book can easily be read in one sitting. It's that good. But I'll tell you how I read it. Every morning I would sit down in my favorite chair with a cup of hot tea in one hand and Rusty's book in the other, and each day I would read a new chapter in the book. It became part of my morning ritual to help me start my day more positively, gratefully, and optimistically. And it worked! Rusty's wisdom touches you like a good friend who puts his hand on your shoulder and says, "You can do it, you've got what it takes, and I love you."

(I'm already encouraging Rusty to get to work on a second volume. You'll see why when you read this book.)

You're holding this book in your hands for a good reason. It's called to you. Now, embrace it, turn the page, and start reading.

I'm reminded of a scene from the movie, "As Good As it Gets," when Jack Nicholson said to Helen Hunt in a pivotal and emotional scene, "You make me want to be a better man." Rusty's book will make you want to be a better person.

I hope you enjoy reading Pee, Poop, Heartache, and Love, and I hope lots and lots of people do, too.

– David J Pollay
Best-selling author of *The Law of the Garbage Truck*
and *The 3 Promises*

Contents

The Calm Before the Storm

Case of Marcal paper towels:	$36.99
Carton of Clorox bleach:	$14.59
Carton of Swiffer Sweeper mops:	$41.99
Two dog beds:	$34.99 each
Three-pack of Sweet Potato dog treats:	$34.99
Thirty-two-pound bag of Puppy Chow:	$35.99

The girl scanning our items at the checkout in BJ's Wholesale Club didn't seem the least bit fazed in our purchase (maybe because our shopping experience wasn't all that unusual to her?). So my wife, Elissa, decided to break the ice.

"We're going to be foster parents for two puppies. They're arriving here this weekend."

"Oh, that is so great of you guys!" After a brief silent pause, she added, "I would love to do something like that, but I don't think I could ever let them go once I loved them—even for a little while."

More silence followed as the last remaining items were scanned.

Elissa spoke up and said that she thinks we can do it. It'll be hard, but we can do it.

And as Elissa was explaining this, I took out my debit card and looked at the total on the register screen. I was thinking that giving them up for adoption will be easy; shopping for them is what's going to be hard!

We started to walk away from the register and the girl yelled out, "God bless you!"

Wow, that was nice. Normally I'm the one saying that phrase to others.

I'm a retired police officer and I became an ordained minister in 2008. Elissa has spent more than three decades as a high school teacher. And we're both animal lovers. We live in a small South

Jersey town where our pets allow us to share *their* home with them. Adding to the mix of family love are my two sons, Matt and Corey.

I retired from the police department four years ago; Elissa retired from teaching last year. I spent the last half of my career as a school resource officer and detective. While I was assigned to the school resource unit, I was offered the opportunity to have a bomb dog. Boomer, a black Labrador Retriever, and I worked together for seven years before he had to retire. He was more than a pet—he was my partner. In the fall of 2009, we had to put Boomer down because his kidneys were failing and he stopped eating.

Watching the medication take effect on my partner of seven years would have brought me to my knees, but I was already lying on the floor with him, holding him well after his body became limp. I know some call it "an act of love," but this felt anything but loving. I knew it was the right thing to do because Boomer was suffering, but that was of little comfort at the time and I battled feelings of guilt wondering if I really did the right thing.

We arrived back at the house and I went right to bed. Even though Boomer had stopped sleeping with us long ago, something felt empty in the house. It was as if his presence was known to me every night when I went to bed. I felt it in our home as we slept in bed and he slept on the floor. And now that he wasn't there, I felt his absence. I couldn't see it, but I could feel it. Does that make sense to you?

We were now a one-dog family with Elissa's dog, Bosco, in the house and I thought that was enough for me. I didn't want to go through what had just happened ever again...

Three weeks later we were driving home from a farm about an hour away with a yellow Lab puppy sitting on Elissa's lap. So much for my resolve to never have to go through saying good-bye to another pet. We named her Bailey, and Bailey and Bosco got along great. And Bailey learned how to get along with our two cats, Bellagio and Bojangles, although that last statement might still be considered a work in progress some five years later.

In the summer of 2012, we had to say good-bye to Bosco. Heartwrenching doesn't come close to the feeling inside the vet's office and on the way home. Watching my wife—my best friend and soul mate—grieve over the loss of a pet she had since before we met was hard; in fact, it was God awful. And that feeling hung in the air in our home for weeks. Hurt, no matter the source, is still pain. And this pain stung, as did the sting of the hurt I felt when I said good-bye to my partner three years earlier.

Eventually things got back to normal, we were adjusting to the change(s) in the house. We were now back to just one dog and both of us were good with that. One dog equals one food bowl, one dog equals one dog leash, one dog equals one load of poop (or two, maybe three), and one dog equals one smelly wet dog to take care of when it's raining.

And one dog means *only* one dog lying in bed with us. Of course the upside to more than one dog is that it increases your chances of blaming one of them when you fart. But since Elissa already professed her love to me, I wasn't worrying about her leaving me because of my farts. Matt and Corey, on the other hand, not so sure. One of the added benefits of having kids is that if the dog's not around (or you're not fortunate enough to have a dog), you can *always* blame one of the kids.

Where were we before I started talking about farts? I think I was trying to lay out a foundation—laying the groundwork—on which to build the rest of this book. I believe I was trying to give the introduction by setting the stage for the pages that follow. And somehow I got the word *fart* in the first couple of paragraphs. Nicely done, don't ya think?

By the way, if you're offended by the word *fart*, and especially the smell of them, you might want to stop now. Yes, I'm an ordained minister, but it's best to keep things real (as Dr. Phil would say). And farts are a part of life. And if you've ever had a dog, you know that farts are part of that life! And let's face it, sometimes life just stinks.

Sometimes it gets stinkier[1]. So does your home. Especially when a bunch of dogs are living in it. If you have a stinky home but no dogs, who do you blame it on? Seriously, if your house smells like wet dog, but has no dogs in sight, there aren't a lot of options; are there? I remember when I was living in an apartment before Elissa and I got married; it was just me and Boomer. Besides keeping me company, he was a great alibi for whatever smells were in the apartment. I can't imagine what lies I would have had to come up with if Boomer wasn't there when unexpected guests stopped by.

So there's the foundation—the groundwork—for the book you're holding in your hand right now. What-a-ya-think so far? Is this something you think has potential?

Well, if you've read this far, you're either interested in it or you're sitting in an airport terminal, your flight is delayed, and you got nothin' better to do for a few hours. Remind me to tell you later about a book I bought in an airport bookstore…

Just take a look at how flatulence has taken us so far off topic! I think when you're a dog person, you kinda get used to this. Whether you're a dog person or not, there's no denying the fact that life gets stinky sometimes. In fact, sometimes life gets downright crappy. But that's a topic for a later chapter. I'd love to be able to sugarcoat it and make it sound less harsh, but that's another part of life that can't be avoided. Life can be harsh, it can stink; and I doubt I'm the only one who's ever thought it gets crappy at times. You don't have to look that far in order to see it—just turn on the news. It's on twenty-four hours a day now, you can turn to your favorite news channel and I bet you won't have to wait more than five minutes before a story comes on, or a talking head starts a discussion on something in life that more than one of us would agree stinks. Or is harsh. Or is…

Ya wanna know what isn't any of those things? Love.

---

1   My spellcheck says *stinkier* isn't a word, but the online Scrabble dictionary says it's an acceptable word for that wonderful board game. So I'm keeping it in the sentence.

Unconditional love is something that we're called to share with one another. The Greek name for this kind of love is *agape*. Roughly translated into English: unconditional love. I can't think of an animal, any animal, that offers that kind of love more than a dog. We humans are supposed to be the ones setting the example, but just turn on your favorite news channel.

So where do we turn if we can't trust the evening news to share stories of this "unconditional love?" Where do we turn to learn about this love? Where do we turn to witness this kind of love? You want to get an idea of where you might find it? Try Googling "quotes about the love of a dog," or "lessons learned from dogs." The first search would reveal more than 45,600,000 results; the second search would give you more than 38,500,000 results. Seems there's something about the love of a dog, wouldn't you agree?

Ya wanna find out what that kind of love looks like in people? Go to your local animal shelter and take a look at what the volunteers do there. Take a walk past the cages and let your heart feel what the people who routinely clean those runs feel in their hearts. Take a peek into the medical room and envision what it must look like when a veterinarian takes a needle filled with a lethal dose of a barbiturate and injects it into the vein of a dog whose death sentence was set simply because he wasn't adopted.

Ya wanna get a sense of what the human side of "agape love" looks like? You need to travel no further than your local shelter. By the way, the word *euthanasia* comes from the Greek words that mean "good death" (a death with a minimum of suffering or distress). Some folks who've had a pet call it the last act of love, the most heart-wrenching kind of love imaginable. Have you ever been there? What if you took a minute right now and went back to that point in time, can you remember the day? Or the days (if you've had more than one pet who had to be put to sleep)?

Does the thought of that good-bye bring tears to your eyes? Maybe it would help to share with you that I have tears in my eyes right now as I'm typing this. I actually just walked away from this laptop and took a break from all this. I wondered if I went too far.

Did I open a wound that shouldn't have been opened or didn't need to be opened. But then I got to thinking that if we're going to be totally honest about things in life, we shouldn't shy away from the bad. Sure, focusing on the good is the best path to take, but I think we need to visit the bad times in order to appreciate the good times more. In fact, I think it's healthy. And so I promise you this from the bottom of my heart: as you cry, I'll be crying, and as you laugh, I'll be laughing. I'll dig deep to reach those feelings in order to see what they've done to us and for us, to help you and me understand that with love comes heartache. As a wise minister once shared at a funeral service, "We hurt so much because we loved so much."

We'd like to love and be loved without running the risk of being hurt (or hurting another). I don't think we can have it that way. We want to love and feel loved, but in doing so we have to open ourselves up to be hurt. In order to love something deeply (perhaps the way a person or animal deserves), we have to be willing to be hurt deeply. Otherwise, that love isn't honest, it's holding back, and sooner or later that kind of love becomes problematic. It doesn't last, does it?

And so we have to acknowledge that sometimes love hurts. And once, a song with that title made it to the Top 10 in 1975! Thank you, Nazareth, for taking The Everly Brothers' 1960 song and turning it into an international hit some fifteen years later. Sorry, I'm one of those "classic rock" people who believe the best music ever recorded was when I was in my teenage years. I was a freshman in high school when that hit from Nazareth was played at the school dances. I'll let you do the math...

Other than going near the topic of euthanasia, have you ever done something out of love that you knew would cause pain? Discipline, maybe? How about taking a splinter out of your child's foot? You knew it had to be done, and yet you knew that you first had to cause pain in order to get the tweezers far enough in there to grab a piece of that bugger. Did you ever need stitches? The medical folks call them "sutures," because maybe stitches sounds like you've gone to a seamstress instead of the emergency room. I can tell you that I've visited our local emergency rooms on regular intervals, mostly when I picked up a tool to complete a project around the house. I almost cut off my finger building nativity scenes for our church. Yes, indeed, sometimes the things we do with love in our hearts cause us pain.

Like the needle they inject right inside the cut (er, uh, "laceration") to numb it, or the orange junk they pour over it—and into it—to disinfect it, or that scrubber that has a sponge on one side and bristles on the other. Yep, I've experienced all of that on numerous body parts over the last couple of decades. You?

Didn't you wish they would just put a big, padded bandage on your boo-boo and send you on your way? That would be less painful, wouldn't it? But what would the end result be? Infection is the first word that comes to my mind. So in order to make sure you and I don't end up with something far worse than we went to the emergency room to be treated for, we have to endure some pain before things get better.

Sometimes we have to be the cause of pain and sometimes we find ourselves being the recipient of pain, but both sides of this pain, as described in the previous paragraphs, are identical in that the purpose is love. The acts of the person are motivated by the kind of love that's concerned for the welfare of another. Without any conditions. Without any reason to get ticked off at them for doing what they need to do, for *doing* an act of love that has very little reward for them. Like the folks at your local shelter. The rewards are intrinsic—that is, it's personal instead of something tangible, like money.

Money can be pissed away, the feeling inside one's heart knowing they've helped someone who was in need can't. Not that everything previously discussed can't put one in a pissy mood; anything that can bring feelings of delight also has the potential to piss you off. Have you ever been there? One minute you're experiencing life's bliss and the next minute you find yourself so frustrated that you could just spit (as my mom used to say).

It's in the spirit of these myriad of feelings and emotions that this book was written—actually, that shouldn't be past tense *was*. It should be present tense—that this book *is being* written. After all, this is just the beginning, just a hint of what's waiting in the following pages. Pages that, as of this point in time, have yet to be written. You want to talk about faith? You've got to have faith if you're going to turn to the next page and then the page after that, because as of yet, there is no "next page." It hasn't been written yet.

Isn't that weird? Even though the next page has yet to be written, there are a bunch of pages after this one that have text on them. Weird, no? You just know my proofreader and editor are both going to be busy editing this and suggesting corrections, especially about verb tense use.

Think about it, I'm writing this as if the pages in the book you're holding are already written. I'm basically living in the future tense. But you're reading it and the book is finished, so all the other pages are complete. In fact, they've been complete for a while now because the process of final draft to first print takes some time. You're essentially reading this in the past tense—it's already been written. And yet, you're reading this right now in the present tense. So to recap, you're presently reading a book that was written in the past, using future tense thinking.

As you soak all that in, consider the title. I think we've covered it all: Pee, Poop, Heartache, and Love. So, that just about does it. Since I covered everything in the title, I guess my work is done.

Nah, there really is a lot more. In fact, I bet when you first held this book in your hands you saw that there were plenty of words on all the pages. And I bet it went something like this: you picked up the book and held it in your right hand, the spine of the book resting in your palm. Your right thumb cradled the back cover, and your other four fingers (assuming you have five fingers) cupped the front cover. Then you took your left hand, grabbed the back cover with your thumb, and then fanned the pages from back to front. (And I bet right now you're looking at your hands trying to see if I described it accurately.)

So you already know what I'm about to promise: there are completed pages in the chapters that follow. And I put my best work into each and every chapter, topic, sentence, and word. And now you get to be the judge. You are now the critic of a whole lot of *Pee, Poop, Heartache, and Love.* And while the title helps set the foundation of this work, there is something bigger than those four words and the subtitle that I hope gives all of us some serious food for thought: The Prayer of Saint Francis.

Take a look at the first line; go ahead, flip back to the first page and take a look at that first line. I wonder how many times that first line has been prayed by people just like you and me, people who didn't consider what it means to be used as an instrument.

Maybe that's a good place to start the rest of the book.

As we took more puppies into our home, dinnertime became an adventure.

Moe and Larry

Lord, make me an instrument of your peace…

Did you ever ask for something and then later, after it arrived, thought that what you asked for might not be the best decision you made? Am I the only who's ever heard the phrase, "Be careful what you ask for"? When we ask "to be used," we have to be willing to accept all the consequences of that request. Take the first line in this oft-repeated Prayer of Saint Francis.

I'm the first one to acknowledge that I don't know a whole lot about St. Francis. For a long time all I knew about him was that he was the patron saint of animals and every year, around the first week in October, there were Blessings of the Animals all over the place. I'm not Catholic, so I only knew this little bit about the saint who is the namesake of the prayer that's the basis for this book you're holding in your hand.

I don't think you need to be a Catholic (in good standing?) in order to understand the meaning of the prayer, basically dedicated to this man from Assisi, who gave up everything he had to start preaching on the streets of his hometown. I don't think you even need to believe in any certain faith or religion in order to appreciate the words and their meaning; in fact, I don't think you need to believe in *anything* or accept any type of teachings in order to see how the idea of these words can affect change in the world.

Even if you don't know the prayer, I bet there's a good chance you've heard some kind of reference to the first line: "Lord, make me an instrument of your peace." Can you see what's going on here? Can you imagine what that means? Giving it all up to be used by someone (even *if it is* God) isn't something that comes natural to us humans. But, oh, how lives have been changed when a few folks did submit to that kind of love. And make no mistake, this is an act of love on both ends—on the asker of this request and on the giver as well.

I get that this is all about love, but why did the writer of it use the word *instrument*? What comes to mind when you think of the word *instrument*? If you have a word processing program on your laptop, you can find synonyms for this word, and what you get are more words like tool, device, utensil, and my favorite: "a thing of implementational value." Now ya gotta admit, that sounds pretty important—a thing of implementational value.

When you think of any of those definitions that are synonymous with instrument, what do you see in your mind? What tool comes to your mind? What kind of device are you picturing? Is the utensil one you find in the kitchen? And what about my favorite synonym, how many "things of implementational value" can you think of?

Or are you a traditional type of person and you're sticking with the word *instrument*? A musical instrument? If you learned percussion in music class when you were young, like me, you're probably picturing a double bass drum set, with a Singerland snare and Zildjian cymbals (maybe one of them is a cool "sizzle cymbal"). If you weren't a drummer in a garage band while you were in high school, you might be thinking of another type of musical instrument.

Getting back to this first line of the prayer, our culture, our society, doesn't take too kindly to the idea of being used. When we think of people who use others in their lives, our blood starts to boil. Okay, maybe that's just me. I just have no time for people who use others for their own gain. I don't care for people who act kind and caring when it suits them just so they can ask a favor. And then they drop that person (or persons) once they're done with them once the need has been fulfilled. It just goes up my butt sideways.

It's one thing to watch it happen to someone else, especially if that person is someone we care about, like a family member or close friend or colleague. And I bet I'm not alone in being able to recall of a situation where I watched this. It's not easy to watch. But when *we're the one* being used…well, that just makes us feel lousy. We feel foolish when we find out just how much we were used, don't we? We get mad, resentful; maybe even vengeful. And those feelings aren't good for us; we know that. We know we're supposed to forgive those who hurt us. Like in The Lord's Prayer: "Forgive us our trespasses (or "debts," depending on your church) *as we forgive those who trespass against us* [emphasis mine].

No one wants to look like a fool. None of us wants to be taken advantage of. So what was behind this line of the prayer? What's it trying to convey? Maybe being used in the early twentieth century (1912 is as far as the original form of this prayer can be traced) didn't have the same negative connotation that it has today? Maybe prayer was different back then?

Maybe it wasn't.

What if this is more than a prayer? What if it was suggesting putting prayer into action, putting *love* into action? St. Francis believed that nature itself was the mirror of God and all creatures were his "brothers" and "sisters." He even preached to the birds and reportedly persuaded a wolf to stop attacking locals if he promised to feed it. Could the man who left his family's wealth (from his father's silk business) behind in order to preach the power of love have had an influence on a prayer that was written well after he died? Was something else in mind other than this prayer being a talking point for sermons?

When we think of love, we think of how it makes us feel; how the actions of another can turn a bad day good. But when we ask God to use us, this idea of love changes. It's not so much about how we're made to feel, but what we're doing to share our gifts. And this giving of love not only changes the person receiving the love. Whatever act of love it is, it changes the giver of love as well. And it can really change the giver in ways he or she never imagined. Especially if the giver asked to be used as an instrument.

Think about it, once used, the instrument is never the same. Whatever list of tools/devices/utensils you came up with, picture them—each one of them—brand new. You just bought it, it just arrived at your home, it was just given to you. Maybe it's even still in its original packaging. Got it? Good!

Now, picture that "thing of implementational value" just before you use it. As soon as you touch it, it's changed. Whether from the oil on your fingers to the depreciation of it once it was taken out if its wrapper, the thing you're now holding has been changed. Now go ahead and use it as it was made to be used: if it's a hammer, there are going to be nicks in it where the head came in contact with a nail; if it's a spatula, there will be sear marks where it came in contact with the pan or the grill; if it's a harmonica, there'll be scratch marks from your teeth; if you envisioned a medical instrument like a pair of forceps, they're going to need to be sterilized again. Now go ahead and think about whatever thing you were picturing and how it has been changed from the very first use. No matter what I'm thinking or what you were thinking, the item(s) pictured in our heads are forever changed once they're used.

What would happen if all of the tools/devices/utensils had a voice and they said they didn't want to be used? If the hammer somehow was alive and refused to be swung, if the spatula said it wasn't going near that hot surface, if the pair of forceps got queasy at the sight of blood and didn't want to go into that heart that was opened up in the operating room? What would our world look like if all the tools in it said they weren't going to be used? If all the instruments refused to be played? If every type of utensil ever invented just sat there on counters in homes, still wrapped in their plastic cocoons that kept them clean?

By the way, who do you think thought it would be a good idea to wrap a pair of scissors in that plastic stuff that's so hard to open you almost lose your religion trying to rip it apart? Am I the only one who curses out the people who think that kind of plastic housing is needed to keep a pair of scissors safe? And how in the hell are you supposed to open that package if you don't have a pair of scissors in the first place? Seems to me that someone had to know that the purchaser of a pair of scissors might not have a pair of them at home, maybe that's why he's buying them! And if that's the case, why would you wrap a pair of scissors in a package that needs a pair of scissors to open it in order to get to them? I can't be the only one, can I?

Taking that entire last paragraph out of the equation, I can't imagine a world where all the things in it didn't want to be used as they were intended. I can't imagine what my life would look like. If a hammer could talk, would it complain that if it was used as intended (getting banged again and again into an iron nail), it would get a splitting headache? If the harmonica had a voice, would it complain about someone using it so bad that it sounded horrendous? (After all, does anyone know how to play the harmonica? I've tried it a couple of times and I don't know whether I'm supposed to blow or breathe in). What if all the spatulas said they refused to get burned? Or the forceps didn't want to get blood on them?

I wonder what would be more distressing: if these things were made but never used, or never made in the first place.

When we're asking to be used, as in the opening line of the Prayer of Saint Francis, we're asking to be transformed ourselves, to be turned into something we never were before that moment in time. And once we agree, we'll never be the same again. Are we ready for that? Are we ready for that kind of change *to us*?

Because when we agree to be used, there's a good chance it's going to cause some headaches along the way. We might get burned. Things might sound horrible. And we might get our hearts broken. Again. And again. And again. But does that mean we shouldn't try? Does that mean we shouldn't take that risk? What about all these questions—and more—with a bunch of dogs thrown in the mix?

When I agreed to foster one little puppy, I was told that's all we would have in our house—just one cute puppy. And I was told this by my wife, who was told this by the owner of the organization we'd be fostering for. I had agreed to be used, not by God, but by an organization that needed homes for dogs that would either spend their lives in a shelter or be put to sleep. This organization rescues dogs and then fosters them (in volunteer's homes) until they get adopted. The foster volunteers take care of them as if they're their own and treat them like family. If you're a home that already has a dog (or two) in it, the fun multiplies exponentially.

When I said I agreed to be used, I probably should have said *we* agreed to be used. Elissa and I agreed to be foster parents. In essence, we agreed to be used in order that a dog might have a chance at life. Little did we know that "one little puppy" would turn into years of fostering dozens of dogs!

> Every boy should have two things: a dog,
> and a mother willing to let him have one.
>
> —Anonymous

Here's how it started:

Elissa and I are animal lovers, we'd both been animal lovers for as long as we can remember. We grew up with pets. We even did a stint volunteering at a wildlife refuge in our town for a little while. As a teacher, my wife helped out the advisor of the school animal welfare club, a club of students who find projects to help with animals. One of their annual events is an adoption fair. Various animal rescues come from all over the area to "showcase" their adoptable pets. And it was at that event that I was invited.

My wife wanted company, I wanted to sleep in on that cold and damp October Saturday morning. And me being the man of the house, I put my foot down, demanded to be heard. And, as King of the Castle, I set the rules—just like every other husband!

So, right after I got done telling her I wasn't going, I got dressed and got in the car. Well, at least I think she heard me.

Imagine you don't care for cold weather. You don't particularly like damp, dreary weather. Now add that to be awakened on a Saturday morning where you weren't feeling that great to begin with. If you're not familiar with the Northeast, October mornings can feel colder than January mornings. Maybe it's because our bodies haven't acclimated to the temperature change. It seems like there are mornings (and days) where you just can't seem to get warm and stay warm. This was one of those days: dreary, overcast skies, temperatures in the mid forties, and just enough drizzle the night before to keep the ground cold and wet.

The adoption fair was set up in the school's parking lot. Thank God the custodians opened the doors to the school for restroom accessibility. Once we got there, that's where I spent the first part of the morning. No, not in the bathroom! Inside the school, walking around trying to stay warm. This was the same school I graduated from (barely), and the same school where I was a school resource officer. I had the master key to the entire school—every door, every office, every room. Even the cafeteria. But we were in such a rush to get out the door, I forgot my keys. So I was at the mercy of the custodians, who, by the way, don't get nearly enough credit for all that they do.

I was so cold I was tempted to grab a broom and work alongside one of the custodians who asked me what I was doing up so early on a Saturday morning. I explained to him what I shared earlier with you: I told my wife in no uncertain terms that I wasn't going to this event with her. He looked at me and, for a moment, no words were necessary; each one of us knew what the other was thinking. He just nodded at me with a sorrowful look on his face, and then he mumbled something about us all being in the same boat. As he walked out of sight, I noticed there was something missing in his step: he was slower, his head hung low, the strokes of his broom were nothing like when I first saw him approaching me down the hall. I think I opened a wound that all of us husbands feel, and now I felt bad about it. And I knew there was nothing I could do, this type of wound can't be healed by words, it takes time. Time and, for some, copious amounts of alcohol. I dedicated the rest of the morning to him, a lone custodian pushing a broom down the hallway of life.

I didn't want to take a chance of ruining anyone else's morning, he wasn't the only custodian working that day. So I bundled up and headed outside. And as luck would have it, I arrived out there just in time to enjoy the goodies that arrived from Dunkin Donuts. In life, timing is everything.

After two cups of coffee (in addition to the two I had before we left the house), I headed back inside. This time it wouldn't be to wander the halls of this sacred educational institution, I had a more pressing (and urgent) need to take care of. The bathroom was warm, warmer than the hallways. I didn't want to leave. But I had to go. Since I already went.

Back outside into the gray. As soon as I got out to the table where my wife had set up camp, I ran into a former student. Now a young lady, she ran one of the rescues in attendance. She and Elissa were talking. Three guesses what they were talking about. Yep, my wife couldn't come up with *one reason* why we shouldn't be a foster family for a rescue organization like this one. And not only did I know this young woman, I knew her father who was also a teacher. And he was standing next to this woman, encouraging Elissa to go along with the scheme that was being plotted. It was almost as if the stars and planets had aligned and fate was working against me. By the time we left the event, there were already cell phone numbers and email addresses exchanged. We were told as soon as the next transport arrived, we would be the first ones called.

Less than two weeks later, my phone rang. I saw who it was. I wanted to let it go to voicemail but my finger hit the answer button anyway. It was her, Taryn, the young lady who I met when she was a high school student, the young lady whose father I knew, the young lady who convinced my wife to get us involved. There was no turning back now!

I was told to be at her house that upcoming weekend. The transport would be arriving Sunday in the late afternoon and we would get an exact time a few hours before they got in. It was now game time. Time to hit the stores and go shopping for what we needed. Or thought we needed. So off we went to the big discount store for supplies. Carrying everything into the house gave us both a reason to look at each other and laugh: what had we gotten ourselves into?

> We keep moving forward, opening new doors,
> and doing new things, because we're curious
> and curiosity keeps leading us down new paths.
>
> —Walt Disney

Just before dinner that Sunday we were officially a foster family for a shelter dogs. Yes, you read that right, it's not a typo; it should have been singular, so I used the "a" to denote a singular item. However, we ended up driving home with two puppies, so I ended that sentence with the plural form of the word, *dogs.* Technically, the entire sentence is correct because we should have been driving home with only one puppy. All I did was combine what I was expecting with what actually happened. Kind of like the way you read the sentence: you were expecting it to end with proper grammar, instead you got something you weren't expecting. Now we're even.

And speaking of even, two puppies entered our front door that evening. This would be baptism by fire. They were greeted by our yellow Lab, Bailey. We weren't sure how she would handle the situation. Lucky for us she saw the puppies as more of a nuisance than a new type of canine snack food with legs.

Before we left Taryn's house we were told their names. Apparently it's not good for foster "parents" to name the dogs they are fostering, as this leads to a situation called "foster failure." It starts with the foster family falling in love with the dog and then instead of allowing other people to come over and see if they like the dog (and therefore want to adopt it), they end up adopting the dog themselves. Basically, the foster family can't bring themselves to say good-bye to the dog because they fall in love with it. So, they "fail" at "fostering," and they [we] become foster failures. And it all starts with the family being able to identify with the dog by giving it a name.

What's in a name, anyway? I guess it's part of who we are, it's who we identify ourselves as. We're given a name at birth and then we're stuck with it. Take my name, for instance. My dad's name was

Russell, his dad's name was Russell…and so, I was named Russell. But we all had different middle names, so at least there were no juniors, and seconds and thirds, and so on. In order to differentiate it from my dad's name and his dad's name, I was Rusty. Not Russ, that was my dad's name. His dad was also Russ. Such a mature sounding name, isn't it?

I actually had a high school teacher tell me if I went with Russ, I could probably be a movie star (well, at least an actor). But she said with a name like Rusty, I would never make it in Hollywood. And you should know that I never once mentioned any ambition to go to Hollywood to her, never talked about having any desire to act; it was just a comment she made about my name. I guess when people read my *given* or *legal* name they don't know what to call me. Is it Russ? Or would you like to be called Russell? When I tell folks my legal name, I'm often asked how many S's in that name? Is that Russell with one L or two? I have to admit, it becomes interesting. And that's why we decided to name our first born, Matthew; we wanted to spare him the excitement.

But a name really does help give us our identity, doesn't it? Like it or not, unless we go through a bunch of legal red tape, we're stuck with the name our parents give us for eternity. In a nutshell, it's who we are. In the Christian faith, when an infant is baptized the officiant asks the parents, "What name have you given this child?" And a lot of ministers (including me) take that opportunity to remind everyone in attendance that the service of baptism helps serve to remind us of not who we are, but *whose* we are. For it's at that moment that many Christian denominations believe that the baptized are claimed as Christ's own forever. In essence, parents and sponsors of the infants are told that we change from who we are to *whose we are.*

And it's at the moment that a dog gets a name that it really becomes the owner's, it belongs to the owner. It changes from just being a dog to having an identity. When we name a pet, we claim it as our own. We take on an awesome responsibility. We assume both the risks and the rewards of being a pet owner. And more often than not, we fall in love with one of God's creatures. And it's very hard to let go of something you're in love with. I guess that's the reason most rescue organizations don't want their foster families naming the animals coming into their homes.

So we didn't get to name the two little Terrier mixes that we picked up that late afternoon. Their names were decided before we got there. They were two of a litter of three that came in the transport, we took two and another family—their first time at fostering as well—took the other one. We got "Moe" and Larry," they got "Curly." I guess if there were a couple more in the litter they would've been named Shemp and Joe...

Moe and Larry were less than three months old and they were loveable and cute. And scared. Imagine being put in a cage, placed in a van, and driven for hours on end to a place you weren't familiar with. No one told you what was going on; you didn't know anyone when you finally got to where you were headed. And you weren't alone; there were dogs from other shelters in that van with you, picked up along the way to where you were now sitting. Maybe a few of us would describe that journey as exciting, but for most of us, I bet words like *scared* and *afraid* are closer to how we'd feel.

And that's just the way Moe and Larry acted when they came into our home—scared and afraid. Especially when they saw a seventy-pound dog looking at them! But Bailey was great and within a few minutes she wanted to play with Moe and Larry out back in the yard. They ran around outside together okay, in fact, they had a ball—Bailey being chased by two little ankle-biters and the two little ankle-biters being chased by Bailey. And boy did they play. They ran around for a while before we brought them all in for a bath.

The ride up to Taryn's house was long and being puppies, they couldn't hold it for the entire trip. We wiped them down as best we could at Taryn's, but they needed to be degreased, literally. We used Dawn dishwashing detergent on them to get rid of the grime from the shelter and the urine and feces from their crates on the ride here. After a round of Dawn, we switched to puppy shampoo for that "just out of the shower, fresh scent" that any dog would long for. Bailey was supposed to get hers first and then we'd attack the foster puppies. Bailey, being a Labrador Retriever, loves water. And she's one of those dogs who loves getting baths.

Imagine a wet, yellow Lab running around a bathroom chasing two puppies who've never been to the second floor of the home they were now locked in. Then imagine a school teacher standing in a bathtub waiting for two puppies to be handed to her. Picture two puppies, shivering because of fear, standing in the bathtub with this teacher who's now trying to calm them down. They finally get calm enough to have lukewarm water poured over them, thereby initiating them to the first step in their first bath.

As the soap began to turn to lather, Bailey decided she wanted in on the fun. Right up and over the sidewall and into the tub she went. Now your mind should be envisioning a woman (a cute one, if I do say so myself), two scared puppies, and a half-dry (or half-wet, depending on your point of view) yellow Labrador Retriever all trying to fit in a standard size bathtub. Add some water, a little more soap thrown in for good measure, and you should have a fairly clear picture of what it looked like the first part of that first night with Moe and Larry.

> First you learn a new language, profanity;
> and second you learn not to discipline your dogs when
> you're mad, and that's most of the time
> when you're training dogs.
>
> —Lou Schultz, trainer of Alaskan Huskies

But wait, there's more! As Bailey was in the middle of her second bath in as many minutes, she decided that was a good time to run out of the bathroom to get her antler. We use deer and elk antlers for chew toys instead of raw hides and things of that nature for her. She enjoys them and they are safer than most products that are meant to be chewed on by a dog. One minor problem: she likes to bury her antler in the covers of our bed. Can you see where this is going?

In an effort to keep Moe and Larry in the bathroom, I swung the door closed; it didn't latch, but at least the puppies, who were soaking wet and still covered with foamy puppy shampoo, wouldn't escape to run through the house. After she found *her* antler in *our* bed, [I guess] she wanted to show it to the puppies. So into the bathroom she trotted, antler in hand—I mean, mouth—proud as anything. She sat directly in front of the tub, her tail wagging back and forth along the rug on the floor, just waiting to be acknowledged. Just as she got the attention of Moe and Larry, Bojangles ventured into the bathroom to see what all the commotion was. Bailey nudged the door open when she came back in with her antler and before I could reach over and pull it shut, our cat, Bojangles, sauntered in.

Anyone wanna take a guess what happened next when Moe and Larry saw Bojangles? Come on, anyone? Someone venture a guess at what it must have looked like when two soaking wet puppies saw a cat for the first time in their lives. On the off chance you're not a gambling type of person, let me fill in some blanks for you: water, Dawn dishwashing soap, puppy shampoo, a handheld showerhead, and one soaking wet high school teacher—all coming together in an effort to catch two puppies who were chasing a cat, who were all being pursued by a Labrador Retriever. The drenched high school teacher was right on their heels.

Bojangles headed for high ground, our bed. The three dripping canines were right behind him. The puppies weren't big enough to make that jump; Bailey, on the other hand, no problem at all. As Moe and Larry jumped up and down on their hind legs trying to get a glimpse of this creature they have never seen before, Bailey was trying to get him to play with her. On our bed. Soaking wet. Instead of playing, Bojangles made a leap for Elissa's dresser along the opposite wall. Bailey was smart enough not to try it. Now two puppies were jumping against the dresser, a dresser that Elissa got from her mother. The high school teacher, soapy lather dripping from her chin, was now yelling at the puppies to stop scratching her mom's dresser. Bailey went back and got her antler, brought it back into the bedroom and got comfy in the bed. I stood there, bent over in laughter. I would later be counseled on how I could've helped out a little more.

I figure someone had to keep a calm head about them, and I decided I was the man for that job. So I calmly grabbed Moe and carried him back to the bathroom. Elissa got Larry and met me in there. Bailey decided to stay in bed enjoying her antler, perhaps enjoying the feel of our bedspread drying her wet fur. It was decided that since she was already soaked, Elissa would jump back in the tub and I would hand her one puppy at a time. Moe and Larry were finally rinsed and dried as best as we could with the towels that had been hanging next to the tub, towels that by this time were so wet they could have been wrung out. We opened the door slowly, tentatively, worrying Bojangles might still be nearby. After we saw that the coast was clear, we scooted Moe and Larry out of the bathroom where they were met by Bailey who jumped off the bed to join them. Elissa gave one look into the bathroom. I wasn't sure if they were tears of sorrow or tears of joy. The walls were soaked, the floor was soaked, wet dog hair clung to every surface and clumps of it were scattered along the bottom of the tub.

Herding squirrels would have been easier...

Next up, dinner. This time for three dogs, not just one. How would Bailey handle this? My former partner, Boomer, was food aggressive and had to be fed separately from Bosco. Moe and Larry combined didn't weigh as much as Bosco. If Bailey wanted to, she could make our two foster dogs a tasty Scooby Snack. Now, for the first time since they came into our house, I was nervous.

Bailey assumed her normal position in the kitchen as Elissa prepared dinner, dinner for the dogs, not for any of us humans in the house. You see, Elissa believes in spoiling a pet rotten, and if that means making them dinner to go along with their pet food, so be it. Ever since we got married I witnessed the ritual of Elissa cooking chicken for the dogs. The baked chicken (most of the time rotisserie cooked) was added to and mixed in with the dog food.

It was only after that blending of various foods came together that the bowl was ready to be placed on the floor. When we came into the picture, Boomer was used to drinking out of the toilet, so this took a little getting used to.

It turned out Bailey didn't care if two puppies were eating near her or next to her, she didn't bother with their bowls of food. However, the same can't be said about Larry and Moe. They scarfed down their food like it was their last meal and then went straight to Bailey's bowl. Bailey didn't show her teeth or growl, she just backed away and let them finish what she left. And then she looked up at us as if to say, "Are you serious?"

To make things even, Elissa snuck Bailey a few pieces of chicken before she put it back in the fridge. This was about the time I saw my extensive dog experience as a benefit to the family. I knew that after you get done feeding puppies there's only one thing to do: put them outside! So back outside the three of them went, and back to the playing and chasing each other in the yard. I stood out there with them while Elissa cleaned up their bowls and started preparing a meal for people to eat. I was hoping Bailey would lead by example—that is, she would show them what they're supposed to do after dinner. I lost sight of them quite a few times and assumed that time was used well. I assumed they wanted some privacy to "do their business" and called them up on the deck after about fifteen minutes. They had their fall coats on, I was dressed in a t-shirt. No one ever said the desire to get warm isn't a good motivator.

> My husband and I are either going
> to buy a dog or have a child.
> We can't decide whether to ruin
> the carpets or ruin our lives.
>
> —Rita Rudner

Once inside the back door, Moe went over to Elissa hoping for another bite of chicken. When she didn't give it to him, he squatted down and peed at her feet as she was cutting garlic. Larry, not to be outdone, went into the family room and took a dump. Bailey looked at both of them, then at us, and walked away into the living room. I guess she was disgusted with everything that just went down. We didn't have time to play Rock, Paper, Scissors to decide who would clean up what, we simply went by who was closest to what mess. I was closest to Larry, Elissa was almost standing in Moe's urine. Instead of paper towels that wouldn't flush down the toilet, I ran into the bathroom and grabbed a handful of toilet paper. Elissa was busy with the roll of paper towels taking care of the kitchen spill, I heading for the family room, game plan in hand.

Did you ever think you had enough of something only to find out you actually didn't? In trying to continue with our efforts to stay environmentally friendly, I took what I thought would be just enough toilet paper from the roll hanging on the wall next to the toilet. Turns out I was wrong. My estimates put it wrong by a good ten to twelve sheets. And this was a two-ply roll.

Either I didn't grab enough toilet paper or the load of crap was bigger than I thought. Now looking back at it, I can't believe something that big came out of a dog that small. Either way, by the time I realized that I miscalculated the whole thing, it was too late. I reached down with the layers of toilet paper in my hand, determined to grab the entire pile in one squeeze of my hand. Again, turns out I was wrong. Instead of grabbing the entire pile, I got maybe three-quarters of it in my hand. And there was one more thing I miscalculated: its moisture content.

Now I was standing, my right arm outstretched; the palm of my right hand facing up. In that hand held the key to this entire operation. If I made it to the bathroom, I'd be a hero (in my own mind), and if I didn't make it to that most sacred of all rooms in any man's domicile, I'd be a complete failure. I didn't even make it halfway down the hallway before I started losing it. And I do mean, *losing it!* Not only did I lose some of the material that was in my hand, I was losing my stomach right along with it. This *mistake* that I was set on cleaning up was wetter than I thought. And if you know anything about toilet paper, even the good stuff is no match for moisture. As globs of Larry's fecal waste was falling along either side of my wrist, I could feel the gooiness of it seeping into the palm of my hand. So yeah, I was literally losing it.

Let's see, did I miss anything so far? Yes, yes I did: the smell of it. I don't know why I thought running down the hall would be better than walking, but it seemed like the right thing to do at the time. Just like the position I held my hand, it was up around chest level, right out in front of me. And that means that the odor wafted gently past my nose because it was at almost the same height. So the faster I ran, the faster it sped into my nostrils. Dry heaves for everyone!

I do apologize for this part, these last couple of descriptive paragraphs. Perhaps it should've come with a disclaimer of sort: "Warning, do not try this at home." However, if you do want to give it a go, may I offer one tip that hasn't been touched upon yet: May I suggest you open the lid to the toilet before you begin. That should be Step Number 1.

So, what had been anticipated as a genius solution on my part to a particularly messy problem turned into a messier of a problem for Elissa to contend with. I was heaving so hard by this point that she felt bad for me and cleaned up the family room on her own. And the hallway. And the toilet lid, the toilet bowl, the top of the tank. And the walls.

We hadn't been home more than three hours and already the house was a disaster zone. But that's okay, isn't it? It's the sacrifices we make for those who are in need. It's the pain we endure without complaining. Basically, it's the price of doing business when that business involves being used as an instrument.

No one has asked what Moe and Larry were doing while all the aforementioned fun was going on. They were in the living room with Bailey, chewing on the leg of the sofa.

Yes, there is a price, isn't there?

But there is Good News: you and me, we're given the chance again and again and again to change and to be changed. The offer is there for us to be used—not for our own good or purpose, but for a greater good and a higher purpose. We can be part of something bigger than ourselves. But it has to start somewhere, it has to start sometime. Isn't today as good a day as any?

Larry on the left, and Moe on the right.

It's amazing what two puppies can accomplish
in a relatively short period of time.

Rocky and Eiko

...Where there is hatred, let me sow love...

Buddha is quoted as saying, "Hatred does not cease by hatred, but only by love; this is the eternal rule." A senior pastor once asked his congregation, "What does love look like?" In 1984, Tina Turner recorded the hit song, "What's Love Got to Do with It?" And seventeen years before that, the Beatles recorded "All You Need is Love."

It's easy to find quotes, songs, and themes about love. Try doing the same for hatred. I'll save you the time, you won't have much luck. Sure there are a few quotes with the word in it, more songs with hate in a lyric or two, but you won't find many positive themes in your search if you're looking for stuff on hate. And rightly so, there's a real negative connotation with that word, it evokes strong feelings.

Depending on what version of the Bible you're reading, the word *love* is used more than two hundred times in the New Testament. Buddha was believed to have lived sometime between the fourth and sixth centuries BCE. That means the idea that love trumps hate goes back hundreds of years before Jesus walked on this earth. Millions of copies of the Prayer of St. Francis were distributed both during and immediately after World War II by a Catholic cardinal from New York and a US senator from New Jersey. The sixties were filled with songs about love (and love itself), and Ms. Turner is one of many singers to bring that theme into the later parts of the twentieth century. And now, a decade and half into the twenty-first century, we're still surrounded by the very idea of love (and equality).

It would seem "love really does cover a multitude of sins" (paraphrasing 1 Peter 4:8). One of my sins is not eating vegetables; I'm not sure I'll ever get to *love* them. In fact, I doubt I'll even get to *like* them. But Elissa never got the memo on this; she insists on putting those green things in front of me at dinnertime. She's so persistent that she's even found ways to try to slip them into some of my favorite meals—her pasta dishes.

Elissa is 100 percent Italian; both parents Italian, totally verifiable. And that means I'm on the receiving end of not only her love, but of her cooking as well. One of her specialties is pasta with garlic and oil. She calls it "pasta oya oya." I call it yummy. Except when she tries to sneak in something green. Like broccoli.

"Hey, hun, do you feel like pasta oya oya tonight?"

"I sure do, how long until it's ready?"

"I just have to cut up the garlic, probably about twenty minutes."

"Okay, call me when it's ready!"

Twenty minutes later, chow time. And I am starving. And although not salivating, one could say my mouth is watering just from the smell of everything cooking on the stove. I don't know exactly what she puts in it, but her garlic and oil makes the entire house smell like an Italian restaurant. So I make my way to the table and what do I see? A big bowl of pasta tossed with garlic and oil...and broccoli! Are you serious? Do you have *any* idea what this means for me?

As Elissa and Corey are enjoying their dinner, I'm making a pile of broccoli on the side of my plate. That's right, I have to go through my pasta and carefully separate the pasta from the green stuff. And when cooked, broccoli breaks apart and you get tiny little green chunks all throughout the dish. It takes me a good five minutes to cleanse the pasta to a level of "edibility" (I checked, it's a real word) that I can eat. In all fairness to her, it still tastes great; in fact, the mixing of the broccoli leaves a certain taste that's not too horrible. Maybe it's all in my head.

Sure, maybe it's a psychological thing with me and vegetables. But who thinks it's a good idea to cook peas with pasta? Especially those little shells? Do you have any idea how long it takes to remove peas from those shells? I'll tell you how long, so long that the pasta is cold by the time you make a pile of them on the side of the plate.

I'm sorry, peas and pasta should never meet—ever. That taste is impossible to not think about. But it's dinner and sometimes you have to give thanks for the gift, not so much how it tastes.

> My dog is half Pit Bull and half Poodle.
> Not much of a watchdog, but a vicious gossip!
>
> —Craig Shoemaker

Some folks just don't have a taste for certain things, do they? And when it comes to dogs, nothing seems to polarize people like "dangerous breeds." Just the mention of certain breeds can cause havoc in an otherwise civil conversation. First up: the Pit Bull. Add a famous football player who plays the position of quarterback, and watch out! Talk about hatred. You either get hatred for the man or hatred of the haters who hate the man who did a stint in a correctional facility for his role in a dogfighting ring.

Before we go any further, let's make one thing clear: this isn't about judging someone. We're not going there; there are plenty of articles written and blogs filled with comments and opinions about that particular incident and person. For the record, I believe in forgiveness. And forgiveness doesn't mean you condone an act; in fact, it has nothing to do with the person being forgiven—it has everything to do with the person doing the forgiving. Forgiveness simply means you no longer hold the person responsible for the debt *to you*; you stop looking for revenge or a payback of sort. Again, *it is not* condoning the act, *it's not* sympathizing with the person, it is simply moving on *for your own good*. But we'll save this topic for the next chapter.

If nothing else, the incident everyone knows I'm talking about brought about conversations on the breed. And the Pit Bull became synonymous with viciousness. People hated the dog simply because of what it was. It didn't matter where it came from, what kind of training it had, or even its temperament; all that mattered was the breed: Pit Bull. People who owned them tried to call them something else, pet owners who adopted them from shelters were forced to lie to their insurance companies or apartment complex managers, and newscasters and talking heads made the breed itself the story.

If a Pit Bull was seen being walked by someone, that person turned and went the other way. Dog parks posted signs prohibiting them, homeowner associations banned them, and judges sentenced them to death. If all the things just mentioned aren't signs of hatred, I don't know what are. But are they signs or symptoms of hatred? As a former paramedic we learned the difference between signs and symptoms of a disease or illness. Signs are physical manifestations of a disease; they can be measured, like vital signs (pulse, blood pressure, rate of breathing, temperature). Symptoms are more subjective; they're what the patient experiences, they have to be described (pain, nausea, itching, dizziness). Signs are definitive indications of a disease, symptoms are characteristics of a disease or illness. Put another way, signs are observations from an objective observer, symptoms are subjective descriptions from the point of view of the person experiencing it.

So what about the Pit Bull? Think about the signs of hatred for this dog. What are the physical, tangible observations you can make? Keep them objective; what have you seen?

Now consider what symptoms of this hatred might look like. What are some of the descriptions that come to mind when thinking about it from the point of view of the hated? What would they say if they had a voice? What would they share with us? How would they feel?

Ask anyone involved with a Pit Bull rescue and you'll hear stories of heartache, ignorance, and finally, when the dog gets adopted, love. For those of you who've taken a chance and threw caution to the wind with your homeowners insurance, you know how much love this dog can give. Sure, you know how strong they are; but you also know how loveable they are.

You have to wonder what next breed of dog will be demonized by the media, and then eventually society. Today it's the Pit Bull, before the Pit Bull it was the Rottweiler, before the Rottweiler it was the Doberman Pincher, before the Doberman it was the German Shepherd. It seems our society is always looking for a scapegoat, something (or someone) to hate. Just take a glance around the checkout line at your grocery store, read the headlines in the tabloids. How many of them incite some kind of hatred?

Who knew that the Pit Bull was once called the "Nanny Dog" because it was so good with children and people trusted them? Perhaps the most famous Pit Bull comes to us from a TV show from the fifties and sixties, *The Little Rascals* ("Our Gang"). Although he didn't have a talking part, he was a beloved character in the shows that aired once a week before the advent of color television. His name was Petey and he was an American Pit Bull Terrier. He didn't look so scary, did he?

In a 2010 Daily Beast website post, an article titled, "The World's Most Dangerous Dogs," listed the most dangerous dogs, ranked in order from #1 to #19.

That article listed the Akita as the fourth most dangerous dog, and the Belgian Malinois as the fourteenth most dangerous dog. In November of 2012, a mixed breed Akita/Belgian Malinois arrived at our house.

> He is your friend, your partner,
> your defender, your dog.
> You are his life, his love, his leader.
> He will be yours, faithful and true,
> to the last beat of his heart.
> You owe it to him to be worthy of such devotion.
>
> —Unknown

Being a retired bomb dog handler meant I had experience with larger breeds. In canine school, when we weren't training the dogs for scent work, some of the guys who had patrol dogs wanted to spend the time in a useful way. In police work it's called "taking hits," and it means you wrap your arm in a piece of leather or burlap and *take a hit* from a patrol dog. Roughly translated, you get all bitten up. If you're lucky, you get to wear a long, padded sleeve on your arm. You still feel the pressure of the bite, but not the intense pain from the teeth. Sometimes you stand there waiting for the patrol dog to take a running leap at you, sometimes you're resisting arrest from the canine officer and without having to be commanded, the dog leaps at you and holds on until you stop resisting. And other times you get a running start, just for the fun of it, and you learn just how fast a trained police dog is. It doesn't matter what scenario you're practicing, you end up on the ground more often than not. They are that strong. And fast. And tenacious.

I'd been doing this fun part of canine training since before I joined the police department. When I was volunteering with the local emergency squad as an EMT, I was asked by the canine officers if I wanted to "help" them do some training. When you're a senior in high school and a couple of cops ask you to do something, you say yes without thinking about it. Thirty years of taking hits comes with its share of stories. I promised not to mention a lot of them because the scars on my body were never reported in an effort to reduce paperwork. A cop is always looking for ways to get out of taking a report; if that means buying another cop a case of beer as a way of saying, "I'm sorry for my dog chewing you up," you accept the offer.

In the short time we'd been fostering (five dogs by this time), Taryn and I shared a lot of our background. So she knew my experience not only working a police dog, but working with trainers (police and civilian) and judging police canine competitions. So her phone call to me wasn't that surprising. A dog was in a shelter in a southern state and was on their euthanasia list. He was going to be put down the next day if he wasn't *pulled* from the shelter immediately. I was informed I was the only one in the organization called. Because of my background, I would be the only one asked. So I asked, "Why?"

The dog in question was a ten-month-old Belgian Malinois/Akita mix and was an owner surrender. That meant his original owner didn't want him anymore so he was dropped off (surrendered) at the shelter. Because of his breed, he immediately went on the shelter's euthanasia list. Larger dogs in that part of the country don't get adopted easily, and since police departments use Belgian Malinois for canine patrol, people in that community don't like them. So his chances of being adopted were slimmer than slim, and to make room for other, *more adoptable dogs*, he would be put to sleep as soon as the mandatory three-day wait expired. We were already at Day #2.

What was I supposed to say? The shelter had no information on him, no idea if he had a history of human aggression, dog aggression, or any other behavior that might make him a difficult placement. When you're told a dog will die tomorrow if you don't take him today, it's almost impossible to say no. At least for us. We figured we'd deal with whatever issues he had when he got to our home. I said we'd take him.

Great, he was arriving tomorrow! Not much time to get ready. Up until that point we'd fostered small little puppies and a medium-sized dog who was docile and easygoing. They were all adopted fairly quickly. Since we had no fosters living with us when I said yes, Taryn took that opportunity to ask one more question: Would we take one more dog from that same shelter? A hound mix had been there since he was a puppy; although not born there, he was dropped off there shortly after he was born. The icing on the cake was a picture she texted me while we were talking. It was a picture of him at the shelter. Is this girl good or what?

Sure, what's one more dog? Time to get into combat mode. Who in our rescue had a large crate? Did we have any large bowls in the house? How about a large dog bed? And what about food? A seventy-five-pound Malinois/Akita mix can eat! Time to head out and do some shopping.

To be fair to Elissa, she never had a large dog, all her dogs were dogs you could carry around if you had to (or wanted to). When I came into her life with Boomer, she had already seen him working at the school where she taught; high school bomb threats means sweeps of the school with bomb dogs. And Boomer was in the school even when he wasn't working, and he got to know all the staff and students. Because I was assigned at that high school, and he was my partner, the students and teachers got to see him every day. Boomer, although big, wasn't intimidating to her. In fact, he endeared himself to her the first summer we were together. Elissa had decided that the hottest day of the year was the best day to weed the gardens in the front yard. Boomer went out with her and took to a shady spot on the porch. I figured if the air temperature and humidity are both in the mid nineties, it's best to stay inside and soak up the A/C. About twenty minutes after they ventured outside, I heard Boomer barking like crazy. I got up to see what was going on and I found Elissa lying on the steps, almost unconscious. Boomer was standing over her, barking to get my attention. After getting her inside and cooled down, I saw that Boomer would not leave her side. And he didn't leave her side from that day on. And from that day on he could do no wrong in Elissa's eyes.

But this time it would be different. Neither one of us knew what we were getting. And Elissa was concerned. Okay, she was more than concerned; she was worried. What would this dog be like? What if he and Bailey didn't get along? As big as he was—and considering his breed—she worried what he could do to Bailey if he wanted to. What if we got stuck with him because no one wanted to adopt him (again, because of his breed and appearance)? What about the other dog we were getting with him, the hound mix? What if he went after him? So many questions that we just didn't have any answers to. And I have to admit, I had some apprehension, myself. Yep, this retired cop, former bomb dog handler who'd taken hits from police canines for decades, was a wee bit nervous.

J'embrasse mon chien sur la bouche!
(I kiss my dog on the mouth)

—Unknown author

We waited for what seemed like hours for them to arrive; a caravan of vans and SUVs were bringing in dogs from along the I-95 corridor to a single family home in the Pine Barrens of southern New Jersey. Finally they pulled up to the house and I saw that Taryn's father, Jay, had the two that we were taking home. He eased his way out of the driver's door of his pickup truck and looked at me with a sinister smile as he was wiping the side of his face. Uh, oh. What had we gotten ourselves into?

Jay made his way over to the rear passenger side and looked back over his shoulder at me again. There were probably a dozen or so foster families there in addition to us; all of them waiting to meet their newest foster dogs. A few of them were first-timers, just like we were a few months earlier. But it seemed like all eyes were on me. What did everyone know that I didn't know? Or were they just curious to see what this dog we were getting was all about? Maybe they had a running bet, a pool going on between just them to see how long it would be before this dog tried to eat me? Whatever was going on, it didn't help alleviate any anxiety I was feeling.

As Jay opened the door, I could see a head peer out. A big head. A head bigger than any other dog head that ever arrived at that particular house since the rescue was in business. The door was opened a little further, just enough for Jay to reach in and grab the leash that was attached to the neck of this animal. One more glance in my direction and then he opened the door all the way. Before he was even invited to come out, the Belgian Malinois/Akita mix launched himself out of the truck and almost pulled Jay over when he ran out of leash. Jay calmed him down and let him empty on a nearby bush. They began walking toward us and then Jay stopped and told us to "watch this." He then got down on one knee in front of this newest rescue and we saw something amazing: All this dog wanted to do was give Jay kisses. I mean wet, sloppy kisses. This feared man-eater got on his hind legs and placed his front paws on Jay's shoulders. He then began licking his face like crazy. It was all Jay could do to get him to stop.

When the love-fest was over, it was our turn. We were told his name was *Eiko* and all he wanted to do the entire trip up to New Jersey was lick Jay's face. There wasn't a crate for him, so Eiko sat in the back seat—at first. That didn't last long and Eiko enjoyed the front seat for the majority of the ride. And being in the front seat, he had access to the right side of Jay's face. When it was our turn to meet him, I was given the end of the leash and told, "Good luck!"

No sooner did I have the leash in my hand that Eiko jumped on my shoulders and began licking me like crazy. The more I told him to stop, the harder he licked. And then I started laughing and before I knew it, I was making out with a Belgian Malinois/Akita mix. My mouth was open as I was laughing and Eiko took that opportunity to insert his tongue down my throat. Sure I'd been accused of making out with a few *dogs* in my early days, but this was the first time it was witnessed by so many innocent people. French kissing a Belgian dog who had part of his heritage in Japan, I guess you could say I became a sort of a world traveler on that afternoon.

> The dog is the most faithful of animals and
> would be much esteemed were it not so common.
> Our Lord God has made His greatest gifts
> the commonest.
>
> —Martin Luther

As I was dealing with Eiko, Elissa helped unload the rest of the dogs, all of them in crates of various sizes. One of the smaller crates had a scared, but friendly brindle-colored dog named "Nathan." There was a brief meeting of the minds and because he'd never been out of a shelter and just needed to be given a chance, we renamed him *Rocky*.

If you remember the movies by the same name, there were a few lines that involved being given a chance. In *Rocky I*, Adrian shares this conversation with Paulie:

Adrian: Einstein flunked out of school, twice.

Paulie: Is that so?

Adrian: Yeah. Beethoven was deaf. Helen Keller was blind.
I think Rocky's got a good chance.

And in *Rocky II*, Rocky tells Adrian, "I'll drive you crazy if you give me a chance."

We decided that Nathan just needed a chance; if given the chance to flourish in a home instead of a shelter, he would turn out to be a good dog. So on that night, in honor of the biggest underdog in American films, Nathan became Rocky.

And just like that, our fears, worries, concerns, and anxieties vanished. Obviously Eiko didn't want to eat anyone, he was more concerned with licking. And Rocky was a friendly dog who ran around with Eiko before jumping in our car behind him for the ride home. And just like on the ride up to New Jersey, Eiko made sure the side of our faces were slopping wet by the time we got home. In fact, it was all we could do to keep him out of our laps during that ride, he insisted on trying to convince us he was a small lap dog who deserved to be riding up front. Rocky seemed to be enjoying both his new name and the back seat where he was just chilling out while Eiko made the ride interesting.

Once home, we made sure to introduce Eiko and Rocky to Bailey slowly by way of a walk. I got out of the car first and Elissa handed me our newest foster dogs. Rocky was unsure of himself and he didn't seem to care much for the leash. Eiko, on the other hand (literally), was full of energy and curiosity. And he got up on his hind legs. Then he placed his front paws on my shoulders and looked me square in the eyes. I couldn't believe we were the same height…

And then, right there in the driveway, he started making out with me again. I wasn't sure if he was happy to be out of the shelter or this was just his nature. But the term *over affectionate* barely scratches the surface when describing his behavior that day. The plan was for me to take Eiko and Rocky a few doors down the street and Elissa would go inside, hook Bailey up to her leash, and then she'd meet us away from the house, in neutral territory. I guess she figured I'd have plenty of time to walk to the next house before she came out the front door with Bailey. Unfortunately, Eiko had other ideas. He seemed happy to continue kissing me instead of heading down the street to christen some bushes in the neighborhood. So when Elissa came outside with Bailey, instead of being in the middle of the street, away from her line of vision, we were just a few feet from her. Things don't always go as planned.

It turned out our concern for Bailey getting territorial with a larger dog on her property was for naught. She saw Eiko as a playmate; she finally had a playmate her size, one that she didn't have to concern herself (or us) with playing too rough or pouncing too hard. This first meeting went great for all three of them. Rocky warmed up to Bailey who was more interested in Eiko's playfulness than his laidback personality. So the walk was more like three kids trying to get to know one another on a playground. Only this time they were hooked up to leashes.

After a walk that finally did include Eiko peeing on what seemed like every tree, bush, and shrub on the street, we headed back to the house. Once inside and off leashes, the three of them started running laps through the first floor: kitchen, into the dining room, through the living room, past the front door, down the hallway, and then back into the kitchen. That constituted one lap. There would be many more laps completed that evening. But we thought that a combined weight of close to two hundred pounds of canine would be better served in the backyard, so out the door they went.

This gave us time to get bowls of water down and some treats ready for when they came back in from their playtime. I'm guessing about twenty minutes went by before we heard them on the deck by the back door. It had rained earlier in the day; in fact, it had been raining steady since the night before. We tried wiping them down with towels. One at a time they were invited inside, Rocky first. He was easy, he stood there nice and calm and let us wipe him down. It wasn't great, but at least mud wouldn't be tracked throughout the house if the laps started up again. And don't forget the furniture, mud doesn't come out of sofas and chairs as easy as you might think. We'd become somewhat of foster experts by this time and we made the necessary decision to sacrifice the older furniture in the family room for the sake of saving the good furniture in the living room. We felt bad about it, but sometimes in life you have to make decisions that involve sacrifices for the better good.

> Being there for a friend is one of the
> greatest gifts you can give.
> Another is allowing them to be there for you.
>
> —Unknown

Eiko was next in the door. He wasn't let in like Rocky, the door wasn't opened by a human to allow him to walk in. Nope, Eiko demonstrated his first act of intelligence by opening the back door himself. I guess he'd decide when he was coming in, not us. He simply stood on his hind legs and pawed at the door knob until it opened. We have those lever-type door knobs throughout the house, including the exterior doors. Eiko simply pushed down on it and the door popped open. And in he ran. And he was feeling amorous once again. But this time he cast his eyes toward Elissa who was standing there with a wet, muddy bath towel in her hand. I think that made her look more desirable in his eyes. By the time his muddy paws landed on her shoulders, his tongue was already going to town on her face. She tried to duck, tucking her chin to her chest. This only got her scalp soaked with dog slobber as he stroked her hair with his tongue. Eiko's back paws left a path of dance steps on the kitchen floor, leaving a trail of evidence where he pushed her around the floor. It was obvious he was leading. She was screaming.

Since the back door was open, there was nothing stopping Bailey from coming in the house. She created the distraction that Elissa needed to escape the love that Eiko was covering her with. When Eiko saw Bailey, he immediately let go of Elissa and ran over to her. And they started playing right there in the kitchen, both still wet and both still with muddy paws, although Eiko's front paws weren't as muddy as they were before he rested them on Elissa's shoulders. After shutting the door, I grabbed Eiko and Elissa took Bailey. We did our best to get the worst of the mud off them, but after taking a step back and surveying the damage, we saw that they all needed a bath.

Anyone remember our first bath experience with foster dogs? Go back and check out that section of the chapter if you need to get caught up. But don't assume we didn't learn anything from that first disaster. Remember, we were now hardened veterans at this. We didn't go upstairs for baths anymore. Nope, we now used the first floor shower—a walk-in shower with a shower door that closes. The system we put in place went like this: Each dog, one at a time, is led into the bathroom. The door is immediately closed behind them. Towels have already been stacked on the toilet lid and at least two large bath towels are spread out on the floor. Elissa changes into old clothes before the start of this. She stands in the shower (equipped with one of those hand-held shower heads with a hose that allows you to spray anywhere you want) and I escort the dog into the stall with her. I quickly close the door behind the dog and then lean against it so it can't be opened from the inside to prevent an unwanted escape. Elissa has the task of cleaning and rinsing, my job is to throw dry towels over the glass wall so she can dry the dog while still surrounded by shower glass. Only after said dog has been dried off is the door opened. I finish the job with another clean towel before opening the bathroom door to release one clean dog.

This process is repeated until every dog is bathed. Streamlined and efficient, that's the way we did things around what had now affectionately been called the Williams Canine Hotel. And speaking of streamlined and efficient, Bojangles and Bellagio learned a few tricks of their own since Moe and Larry got adopted. For example, they'd become experts in judging the distance needed to outrun any new foster that arrived. They developed this keen sense of awareness of exactly how far they needed to be from any given dog in the house, and that distance varied with each dog. They knew every dog was unique and they quickly adopted strategies to deal with each temperament and in particular, speed of each foster. That continued with Eiko and Rocky.

Rocky, being the laidback dude that he was, allowed the cats to be as curious of him as he was of them. In fact, it's safe to say that they were more interested in him than he was in them. Eiko, on the other hand, he was *definitely* interested in what they were all about! However, all it took was a couple of whacks from the paws of Bojangles to his face and Eiko decided it was safer to stick with dogs than cats.

Hey, remember when I added up the total weight of the three dogs as they were running around the house? Great, now take that and divide it evenly by the area of a queen-size bed. Add in two humans to get a mental picture of that first night with Rocky and Eiko. Just make sure you leave room for two cats who jumped onto the bed in the middle of the night. Actually, make that jumped *into* the bed in the middle of the night. Elissa woke up to find Bellagio under the covers curled up against her legs, Bojangles took a special liking to my pillow.

So there we were, one big happy family. Two cats, three dogs, and two humans who had no idea how it all came to this. At least I didn't have to go to work the next morning; Elissa's alarm went off as it does every morning (and has for the past thirty-five years) at 4:50 a.m. She got up, I stayed in bed.

> As soon as you concern yourself with
> the 'good' and 'bad' of your fellows,
> you create an opening in your heart
> for maliciousness to enter.
> Testing, competing with, and criticizing others weaken and
> defeat you.
>
> —Morihei Ueshiba
> (Founder of Aikido)

Martin Luther King, Jr. once said, "In the end, we will remember not the words of our enemies, but the silence of our friends." I have to wonder how many of us stay silent when we should be speaking up. What holds us back from doing the right thing? Why do so many people stay silent when they witness acts of bullying?

Of all the terms that evoked feelings of fear and intimidation in the dog world, the branding "bully breed" has to be up there at the top. It wasn't always that way, in fact, prior to the 1980s that term for dogs can't be found (this according to Animal Planet's website, discussed on a link to pets, "What is a Bully Breed?"). Our society will stand by and watch bullying of people, but just the mention of a *Bully Breed* dog and you get folks coming out of the woodwork to speak their minds. If it's a dog that sounds scary, we want nothing of it in our community. What would our world look like if we sowed love where we saw bullying? Bullying in our schools and playgrounds as well as dogs classified as bully breeds?

Can we sow love where there is hate? Can we plant seeds of love where we see disgust? Can we put our fears aside to show love to someone (or something) who's been labeled as bad or dangerous?

It's not easy; it won't be easy. You finally take that risk and before you know it, you're making out with a seventy-five-pound dog!

Hatred doesn't always have to be an overt act or statement. It can be hatred by omission. Ignorance, apathy, laziness, or even boredom, they're some of the ways we deal with things we're not comfortable with. When we don't understand something, we have two choices: learn more about it, or dismiss it. One takes work, the other involves doing nothing.

What happens when we do take time to learn more about something that we don't understand? When we put our preconceived ideas aside and take it at face value? When we don't formulate an opinion until we have all the facts? What *would* (future tense) happen if we took the time?

I doubt I'm alone in searching for facts to support my opinion. Sometimes my opinion is strong, and I need as many facts as possible to engage anyone who might disagree with all the knowledge on the subject that's stored in my powerful—and all-knowing—brain. I'll tell ya, it really is easy to get caught up in ourselves, isn't it? Can you imagine what our lives would look like if we gathered all the facts *first*, and then came up with an opinion about something? Instead of searching for only the facts that support our way of seeing something, what if we searched through *all* the facts available and then made a decision on something?

History is riddled with hatred, persecution, and oppression of people because of the way they looked. Rumors (unsubstantiated) have directed actions against groups of individuals who were guilty of nothing other than what was told about them. Fear has driven us to wars with peoples from other countries who were killed because of their beliefs. Misunderstanding before knowing all the facts (a definition of prejudice) has caused more harm than could be written in all the books in all the libraries in the world. And yet it continues.

You have to wonder what dogs would say (assuming they had a voice) about us; how would they treat us if they acted on everything they heard about us? What would they say to each other about us humans if they heard all we want to do is harm them or use them for our benefit? How lucky are you and I that all a dog sees is love?

And how lucky are we that we get to feel something that we never dreamed of happening? Yep, we can feel the love of one of God's creatures that just needed a chance, or the paws of a gentle giant on our shoulders. Just remember to keep your mouth closed when the love fest begins...

There is Good News for all of us, good news in the form of understanding—understanding that we don't have to look the other way, we don't have to feel compelled to go with the crowd because of fear or ignorance. You and me, we have a chance to take hatred and turn it into something special. We can turn hate into love. And in doing so, we have an opportunity to demonstrate to God and to our neighbors that love is more than a feeling, love is an action.

Eiko (in the foreground) and Rocky (behind him) stare out
the window as they ponder life in their new home.

Eiko, the resourceful one, uses Rocky as a pillow.

Reptar

Ever been hurt? Ever been the hurt-er? If you can read this, that means you're probably older than a fifth grader. And that means you've lived a life filled with joy and sorrow, sickness and health, pleasure and pain. That last couple there can be the hardest, can't they? Those last two comparative words: pleasure and pain, seems we're continually trying to find ways of grabbing one and avoiding the other. We can be the receiver of either word, or we can be the giver of them.

I learned a long time ago not to ask a woman her age, so on the assumption that there's a fifty-fifty chance that you're a lady reading this (or know someone who is a lady), I'm not going to ask your age. It's the least I can do. But the issue brought up in the previous paragraph can't be ignored. None of us have gotten this far in life without being hurt. And none of us have gotten this far in life without hurting someone. It's just the way it is. It might not be fair, but who said life is fair? Who was it that said, "Life's not the way it's supposed to be. It's the way it is..."?

If you've been hurt, you want some kind of retribution. I know if I've been hurt, I look for a day of reckoning for whoever caused the pain. Yeah, I know; I'm a minister and I shouldn't be looking for revenge. I never said I wasn't real; I might have been ordained into the Christian ministry, but that doesn't mean I stopped being a human. Look, I'm still working on things, okay? I have a lot of baggage; I lived a lot before the whole "calling" thing happened. And I have to tell ya, I tried to avoid it; I looked the other way. In my book, *Can I Get There From Here?*, I mentioned that I kept saying no, but He wasn't taking no for an answer. I kept insisting that He had the wrong guy. Eventually I caved and took Him up on the idea. I'm not sure if He's rethinking His idea or not. I know I'm not, but I guess you could say I'm still a work in progress.

How about you? Are you still working on things in your life that would make it better? Working on things that would make you a better person? Me too! And one of them is not looking for paybacks every time I've been hurt, not seeking revenge. Not making sure justice is served each and every time. You?

> To err is human; to forgive, canine.
>
> —Unknown

Why is forgiveness so hard? We all want to be forgiven when we screw up, we all look for compassion and understanding from the one who's been hurt. Forgiveness is a theme in every major religion; it's important for society in general. Some might say it's needed in order for society to function at all. Here's a question that just popped into my head: If we all want forgiveness, if we all feel we deserve it at some time or another, if we all want to be the ones being forgiven, who are going to be the ones doing the forgiving? Imagine a world where everyone is forgiven but no one does the forgiving.

Strange, isn't it? When I meet with couples before they get married, I ask them what would happen if someone made their future spouse look like a loser. I probe deeper and ask them how they would react if someone made their future spouse *feel* like a loser. You probably wouldn't be surprised at the answers. Some of them can't be shared here! No one wants their loved one to look like a loser, no one wants their partner to feel like a loser. Not one of us would stand by and allow it to happen.

After we agree that neither person would allow that to happen, I ask them how they settle arguments. How do they get their way? I then ask them this question: "If you go out of your way to win every argument, what are you automatically making your partner?" After a brief pause, in that moment when they "get it," I try to explain the futility in winning every argument. Because, in a relationship, if we're good at finding ways of winning, that means the opposite is also true: we are good at making the other person a loser. And we do become good at it! But if we wouldn't stand by and allow someone else to do it, why do we do it? Why do we feel we have a license to hurt the very person we're about to marry? It doesn't matter if you're in a relationship or not, you can relate this concept with those in your life that you care about. We all can. It doesn't matter if we're getting ready to be married or not, the idea of making someone we care about a loser doesn't sit well.

That basically sums up my marital advice to couples. The rest of the time we talk about their lives, their dreams, their expectations, and their worries. At the end of the meeting I give the couple a calculator, a cheap one I usually pick up on the way to the meeting (hey, I'm retired and it's not like I have a ton of money sitting around for a nice wedding gift). Before I surrender this precious token of my hopes for them, I remove the battery from it. I suggest that they keep this calculator handy, maybe leave it in a conspicuous place in their home. And I tell them to never put a battery in it, never even think about turning it on. Because, I explain, if each one tries to calculate how much they're giving or how much the other owes in the relationship, it'll never work. In short, don't keep score.

End of marital advice for any couple thinking of getting married, for those in a relationship, and for anyone looking for happiness in their home.

> Never let the odds keep you from pursuing what
> you know in your heart you were meant to do.
>
> —Satchel Paige

If October mornings in New Jersey can be cold, damp, and nasty, imagine a rainy night in December. Around ten o'clock I received a call from Taryn explaining a peculiar situation that she only trusted me with. Another dog she knew little about, and one that was abandoned in a home a few towns away from ours. And once again, my background in handling large dogs and dogs with aggression issues made me the perfect foster to place this animal. It's hard to say no when you hear a family packed up and moved and left their dog tied to a tree in the backyard.

The deal Elissa and I had by this time was that neither would agree to accept a dog into our home without first checking with the other and discussing it. But the tone of Taryn's voice told me this was, quite literally, a "do-or-die" situation, and before I could say, "Let me check with Elissa," I heard the following words come out of my mouth: "I'll meet you there in thirty minutes."

Elissa: "Who was that?"

Me: "Oh, it was Taryn."

Elissa: "What did she want?"

Me: "Huh, what?"

Elissa: "What did Taryn want to discuss at this time of night?"

Me: "Oh, just a situation with a dog."

Elissa: "I heard you say you'll be there in a half an hour; where are you going?"

Me: "Yeah. [long uncomfortable pause] I'm going to go steal a dog with her."

Elissa: "You're gonna what?"

Me: "I'm meeting her at an abandoned house where a family left their dog tied to a tree."

Elissa: "And then what?"

Me: [another long pause] "Have I told you lately how much I love you?"

After apologizing for making this decision without her, it was decided that I'd have a family accomplice on this mission: Corey. The youngest son was chosen to drive me to the home where we'd grab a dog we knew very little about. It seemed the best option at the time since I don't drive at night because of all the medication I take for pain. After she agreed to have Corey drive me, I told her of another reason he might be needed…

There was a *slight* chance we might have to break into the house to get the dog. The neighbors had been feeding him and talked about getting him out of the weather. Corey grabbed his coat quicker than Elissa could stop him. There's something about the adventure of helping your dad commit a felony, in this case breaking and entering, that motivates a nineteen-year-old to drop the game controller and move faster than you've ever witnessed.

On the drive there, I explained to Corey what we knew: A retired couple abandoned a house and moved away. They left their Australian Cattle Dog tied to a tree in the backyard, and the next door neighbors had been feeding it. The neighbors called someone who called someone who knew of our rescue organization. Taryn took the call and worked the chain of "notifiers" back to the neighbor who gave her one of the couple's cell phone number. Taryn got a hold of the husband who verbally gave his consent to take the dog. He explained they simply couldn't care for it anymore as they ran into hard financial times. A deal was made that if he allowed us to take the dog, we wouldn't report him to animal control. He told her the dog's name was Reptar and he *should be* okay with strangers.

That was it. Corey was now up to speed on everything Taryn and I knew. Well, mostly everything; I didn't see the need to explain to my son that there was no way to verify who Taryn actually spoke with, it could have been anyone, for all we knew. The neighbors were so upset when Taryn talked to them, they could have given her any phone number just to see this dog taken care of. The sound of the windshield wipers was the only noise either of us heard the rest of the way there, I think we both went into that place where you run a bunch of scenarios through your head. Mine included adding up all our bank accounts to see if the sum total equaled the amount I estimated the bail would be if a different neighbor called the New Jersey State Police upon seeing us removing a dog from a house. In the pouring rain. In the dark of night.

We met Taryn in an unlit parking lot that was directly behind the property. From the parking lot we had an unobstructed view of the rear of the house. The plan was this: Taryn and I would approach the dog. Taryn had a leash in her coat pocket and would hold onto the handle of it, and I would be responsible for hooking it to Reptar's collar. If he attacked us, Corey was our backup and would use whatever was handy to pry Reptar from either (or both) of us. The three of us, already soaked from the forty-degree pouring rain, approached the yard quietly. We saw the line extending from a large tree, but no dog at the other end of it!

There was a shed at the rear property line and we thought Reptar might be in it. I was nominated to check it out. The sound of rain pelting the shed roof helped mask the sound of my heart pounding. During my twenty-five years as a cop, I approached a structure like this dozens, if not hundreds of times, and never did I remember feeling this level of apprehension. Maybe that was because in each one of those previous "tactical approaches" I had a 9 mm handgun on my side. And I didn't have my child a few feet behind me.

Waiting for a bad guy to lunge at you is what police officers train for; waiting to see if an angry dog is going to chew you up is not what I was trained for. Lucky for me the shed was empty. Now the question turned to where he could be hiding. As all three of us were checking the rest of the yard, a dog started barking from inside the house. Taryn went to the neighbor's house to see what information she could get and Corey and I stayed at the back door. The dog inside, presumably Reptar, was barking louder and louder. The barks seemed to be getting more aggressive as if this dog was protecting its property and we weren't welcome.

Taryn was only gone a few minutes before she returned to meet us under the shelter of a small roof covering the back step. She learned that the neighbors were so upset that Reptar was outside in the cold rain, they put him inside the abandoned house. They told Taryn that we could go in and get him; they received permission from the owners. With that information, we pulled on the back door. It was locked. We went around to the front door, it was locked. Time for a different approach.

As Reptar (now confirmed it was him) continued vocalizing his displeasure with our presence, a different neighbor walked over and met us on the front porch. She said Reptar was a nice dog and she hadn't heard of any reports of him biting anyone. Well, that was a bit of good news on an otherwise gloomy situation. Now, the louder Reptar barked, the more outside lights that went on up and down the street. We were causing a commotion.

Taryn went around the house to see if any windows were open. Corey stayed with me on the front porch and watched his father jimmy a double-hung window open. A proud moment of handing down an important skill from one generation to the next. By the time Taryn came back around to the porch to tell us we'd have to break a window, I had the sashes separated and we were peering in through an old set of mini blinds that hung at the living room window. From what we could see between the slats, the house was left a mess.

The *breaking* part of this crime was committed when I jimmied the window; the only thing left was the *entering* part. Once that was completed, we'd have ourselves a full-blown breaking and entering felony to add to our resumes. The only question was who was going through the window. Taryn looked at me and I looked at her. Then we both looked over at Corey. He was younger, thinner, and in better shape than either of us. And since he was younger, he was probably quicker too. He knew what we were thinking without us having to say a word. He nodded in agreement and began to reach for the window. Before he could climb in, I grabbed him and reminded him of what he was already taught growing up with dogs.

1. Don't make eye contact with him.

2. Don't make any sudden moves.

3. Take it slowly, there's no time limit.

4. Speak softly, but only if you have to.

5. If he comes at you to attack, give him your arm (dogs will most often go for the closest thing to them when they're attacking).

6. Do not get your face close to his.

7. Stay calm.

"Yeah, Dad, I know. Don't worry."

Sure, no worries whatsoever. My flashlight illuminated the room and we could see Reptar in the hallway, just past the living room. Taryn and I boosted Corey through the open window and his foot got caught on the blinds as he fell over the couch that was under the window. So much for no sudden moves. Do you know how hard it is for a father not to laugh at his son falling over a sofa, bringing a set of mini blinds down on top of him?

I yelled in the window for Corey to be careful. So much for speaking softly. I caught myself yelling, so I changed to a whisper telling him to go unlock the back door. All I got in reply was a thumbs-up with his back to me. He was staying focused on a dog that might or might not attack him. Good boy! (Corey, not Reptar).

Taryn and I rushed around back hoping not to hear any screams coming from inside the house. Corey unlocked the door and we went in. To our surprise (and relief), Reptar was sitting in the kitchen, and Corey didn't seem to have a care in the world. "Look, Dad, he's fine. See, he even lets me pet him." I had hoped Corey wouldn't have gotten that close to his face, but Corey had an instinct and went with it. He tried kindness and Reptar responded.

I went into the living room and locked the window, then we hooked Reptar up to the leash and walked out the back door as if nothing happened. But like any hardened criminal knows, time is your enemy and I still didn't know if we were clear. Someone still could've called the state police and they might be on their way right then and there. I know response times can vary depending on call volume and manpower. I didn't want to push our luck and try to explain that based on a phone call to an unconfirmed person, we entered a house that wasn't ours and took something that didn't belong to us. And I seemed to be the only one concerned about this. Maybe I was simply thinking about how embarrassing it would be, as a retired cop, to convince my brothers and sisters in blue that nothing we used as permission to go and get this dog was able to be confirmed in any way.

I packed my jacket pockets with dog treats before we left our house. I figured they could be used as a bribe in the car on the way home, a deal between me and Reptar that as long as I fed him he wouldn't try to eat us. And it worked! Corey drove and I handed treats back to Reptar who was sitting in the back seat. One treat at a time, I was bonding with a dog who was left to fend for himself in an abandoned home. My only worry was that I'd run out of treats before we pulled into the driveway.

> I've seen a look in dogs' eyes,
> a quickly vanishing look of amazed contempt,
> and I am convinced that basically
> dogs think humans are nuts.
>
> —John Steinbeck

I was hoping the rain would stop before we got home. We still had to assimilate Reptar with the rest of the pack. And that involved going for a walk with each dog. We had this routine down to a science by now: the new foster dog would be let out of the car and walked a few houses away. Then, one at a time, the pack members would be taken for a walk with the new foster. This was done so that the meeting of the dogs took place in a neutral territory— the street, away from our house. That way no one felt they had to protect or defend or claim their territory. The meeting was simply two dogs seeing each other for the first time in a place that meant nothing to either one of them.

Bailey was always the first dog of ours to meet the newest fosters. This helped cement her role as pack leader among the dogs. She was alpha and everyone knew it. Even Eiko! She had a way of letting each dog know who the leader was. It never led to a confrontation, it was as if each dog just knew. And if the puppy fosters were playing too rough with each other (in her eyes), she would go over to them and pounce at them while barking. It was her way of saying, "Settle down!"

Unfortunately, the rain kept up and the temperature stayed in the low forties. Corey took Reptar down the street and I went in to get Bailey. Being a Lab, she loves water, even if it's rain. The rest of the dogs think she's crazy, they have no desire to go out in the rain. Bailey and Reptar's meeting went great and other than the usual sniffing of each other's butt, we walked at a fast pace so we could get inside and get warm (and dry!). Next up, Eiko; then Rocky. Both seemed to have no problems with Reptar; more butt-sniffing and a few playful nudges with their snouts were the only distractions on those walks. Our other foster, Spirit (a Lab mix), was the most submissive of the dogs we had in our pack at the time. She came out and she and Reptar seemed to hit it off instantly. No problems whatsoever.

Sounds simple when it's explained that way, doesn't it? In order to appreciate the amount of time it actually takes, you have to understand how we walk the dogs so there's a lesser chance of aggression. It looks something like this:

(newest foster) (human) (human) (current Williams Canine Hotel guest)

Do you see how there are two people between the dogs on the outside? Each person walking the dog makes sure their dog is to the outside. At first. Once the dogs are walking okay in that configuration, we switch it to this:

(newest foster) (human) (current Williams Canine Hotel guest) (human)

This way of walking them is an "every other one" type of situation—human, dog, human, dog. Once that way of walking goes smooth, we switch it again, to this:

(human) (newest foster) (current Williams Canine Hotel guest) (human)

Now look what we did. We put the dogs in the middle and people at either end. This is the real test to see what happens when two dogs that don't know each other are walking side by side. You can see that it takes some time to get to this point. First, it's a dog, next to a person, next to another person, then a dog on the other end. Then, it's a dog, next to a person, next to a dog, next to another person. The dogs are getting closer together, but there's still a human between each one. Finally, we get to the point where it's a person, next to a dog, next to a dog, and another person on the other end.

We always end each walk in the front yard to see if there's any reaction to dominance or territorial aggression. But that's not all we do before the new foster dog comes inside; we have to see how the newest member of the pack walks with another dog with just one person. That's right, one of us grabs two leashes attached to two dogs. And away we go. This is the final test to make sure there won't be a problem inside. Plus, the structured walk helps cement who's in charge—us humans. And it gets the dogs focused on something other than each other.

To figure out how long this takes, multiply everything I just explained by the number of dogs in the house. And in this case, in the rain as well. Since I have the most training, I'm usually the one doing that last walk, the one where one human walks two dogs at a time. Or three. Sometimes four. Once in a while five. And every so often, six. All at one time, together as a pack, walking down the street. Some of our neighbors think we're crazy...

Finally inside, all the dogs should be tired from the walks. But they're not, they're excited that a new dog made its way into our home. They want to play, they want to get to know each other. Corey wants to get warm. I want to go to bed. Elissa wants to cook for them. Not until tomorrow, hun, save it for tomorrow. Please? And just like that, we were in bed. All of us. In bed. Together. Each dog slept like a baby, I slept like a dog. In the morning it was breakfast time.

> If dogs could talk, perhaps we would find it as hard
> to get along with them as we do with people.
>
> —Karel Capek

And that's when all hell broke loose. Bowls were filled, and water was freshened up. Eiko went to his usual place in the kitchen and waited, Rocky went to his place, and Spirit went to her place. We set a place for Reptar at the other end of the kitchen. And Bailey waited right at Elissa's feet as the first to be served. No sooner had all the bowls been put down when Reptar took off toward Eiko. Eiko, who had just started eating, looked up and I saw the hackles go up as he made eye contact with Reptar. Reptar appeared to be in a trance and he lunged at Eiko and they went at it. They went at it hard. Elissa instinctively reached down to grab a tail, but was unable. I ran over and grabbed Reptar by the tail and pulled him away from (and off of) Eiko. Elissa stepped between the two and tried to restore calm. I hadn't gotten up to Reptar's collar with my hand and his tail slipped out of my hand. He was right back at Eiko. But this time Elissa was between them.

She screamed, loud enough that I heard it over the brutal barking. When I got to her, Elissa was holding her lower leg, in the area of her calf. Her scream startled the two combatants enough that I was able to grab Reptar and put him out the back door. When I went back to Elissa she was sitting on the floor, holding pressure on her leg. There wasn't a puncture wound, but teeth marks were clearly visible on her leg. And she was now running late for work.

I was given the task of trying to repair the damage in the pack. I worked all day on *resocializing* the pack, paying particular attention to Reptar. After a few nice walks together, I let Eiko and Reptar out back together to see how they responded to running freely without any food to protect (or go after). It took less than five seconds for them to be running and playing together like two best friends. Eiko found a stick and brought it over to Reptar as if to say, "Ya wanna play?" Reptar grabbed one end of it and they started a playful tug-of-war. But the stick was no match for those two pairs of jaws and soon the stick was nothing more than a pile of splinters. I'd seen enough and decided the rest of the pack should be able to get in on the fun.

The sight of five dogs running free together as a pack is something that's hard to describe. They were all free to be the animals that they were. Bailey was in charge and everyone followed her lead. Wherever she ran, the rest followed; whatever stick she picked up, the other dogs wanted; wherever she peed...

Fifteen minutes later they were all back inside and their reward was a dog biscuit. Each one of them had to first sit and then they'd get their treat. First Bailey, no problem there. Next, Eiko. Again, no problem, and Reptar didn't show any interest. Phew! Rocky, Spirit, and Reptar all took their treats calmly and everything was once again okay. For a little while.

A few hours later I had "the pack" resting in the family room, each one claiming a place on the couch and love seat. Except Reptar. He decided to lie on the floor in the kitchen with a view of everyone. I turned on the TV and sat back to watch a little ESPN programming. I couldn't tell you how long it was, but there came a point in time when all hell broke loose *again*. Eiko was doing nothing but lying on the couch, scanning everyone (including me) like he's always done. His eyes met Reptar's eyes and that's when Reptar launched from the floor and darted at him. Next thing you know, dog fight, round 2. Since I saw who the aggressor was I went after him in hopes the nonaggressor didn't want to fight in the first place.

I grabbed Reptar's collar and yanked him away from Eiko. Eiko looked at me like he was trying to tell me something. I "escorted"

Reptar out the back door and went back to check on Eiko. No blood, just a little bit of fur on the floor. What the hell just happened? What set him off?

Reptar was brought back inside and we tried something different, this time we'd remove all the other dogs with the exception of Reptar and Eiko. Minutes passed, and they were fine; minutes turned to hours and they were playing together. The other dogs came back in and everyone got along great. Elissa came home from school and made sure she gave Reptar the same affection she gave the other dogs. There wasn't a grudge held; all was forgiven between Elissa and the dog that left a huge bruise on her leg.

Dinnertime came again and this time Reptar was fed in another room, cut-off from the rest of the house with a gate. Dinner was served without incident. A glimmer of hope, a step in the right direction. Bedtime came and the dogs slept together as if they'd known each other their entire lives.

Our second full day with Reptar started off the same as the first, with the noted exception of where he ate. Elissa was once again off to teach impressionable young people web design, computer applications, and graphic design. I was hoping to have a day designed for relaxation. It started off great and lasted into the afternoon. It lasted to dinnertime and beyond. It lasted right up until it didn't.

Right around late-night snack time the fecal matter hit the rotating oscillator ventilator. Once again all it took was Reptar to make eye contact with another dog, this time Spirit, and it was game on. Spirit didn't know what to do. I knew I had to do something. I jumped in, I had to protect a dog who was way outmatched. In doing so, I got nailed on the arm. It happened when I reached in to separate Reptar from Spirit. I knew I made a mistake, I knew I should've reacted the way I was trained. Instead, I instinctively reached between two dogs going at it. And as a result of my stupidity, I got tagged pretty good. Maybe Elissa and I could now compare bruises. Mine would include a few puncture wounds.

This behavior continued on a regular basis until Taryn and I made the decision to "rehome" Reptar with another foster family. Maybe a change of environment would help. It was a sad, but necessary decision—sad because Reptar was a real lover with the humans in our home, and 90 percent of the time he was great with the other dogs. But that other 10 percent caused havoc and put other creatures in danger. The next foster family to take Reptar had similar issues and one of their children was bitten in a melee involving Reptar and one of their dogs.

Now it was getting to be decision time; now as a trustee with the organization I was involved in very difficult decisions. A trainer, on staff with our rescue, had been consulted early on in the days of Reptar. He had been made aware of each incident and made recommendations each time. Without meeting Reptar, he thought Reptar deserved a chance before making a decision that would be a permanent one. He made room in his home for Reptar and worked with him, one on one, until he believed Reptar was ready to be adopted.

After a few months of being at this trainer's home, Reptar was adopted by a mature couple who had no children and no other pets in the house. Reptar would be an only child type of dog. And you should know that he's thrived in that home ever since.

Reptar went after every dog he ever met. And yet, each of those dogs played with him afterward. Every dog went out back and ran around with him, every dog came back inside and shared a sofa with him, and every dog acted no different toward him after one of the many conflicts.

Elissa came home from work the day she was bitten and made sure Reptar was okay. She wanted to make sure he knew he was still loved. He was not treated differently than any other dog. I'm not sure if I could be so forgiving of a dog who left a bruise and swelling that's still noticeable today. I tried, I really tried to be understanding, after all, we didn't know anything about Reptar when we got him. We didn't know his background or his medical history. I tried not to be judgmental, but he hurt my best friend, he injured my bride. It took a lot of work and a lot of thinking, scrutiny of my beliefs and values. In the end, I had no choice but to forgive Reptar.

Forget injuries, never forget kindness.

—Confucius

Why did the dogs just "get on with their lives" after each incident? Why didn't they hold a grudge? How could they possibly trust Reptar again? And, hey, why was it that Elissa forgave him so quickly for hurting her when I got the cold shoulder for days when I bought her a vacuum cleaner for her birthday? Look, she said the one we had wasn't picking up all the dog hair, and she said her life would be so much easier without so much dog hair. What husband wouldn't take that as a hint and go out of his way to make sure his wife's life was easier?

There is a lesson in this story, no? I'm amazed by the amount of love shown by dogs. I'm embarrassed that sometimes they seem to "get it" more than us humans. What would you take away as one lesson from the way Reptar was seemingly forgiven by everyone he hurt? Two families had their lives turned upside down and both not only forgave Reptar each time, members of each family went out of their way to work with Reptar in an effort to help him. How many of us would be so forgiving?

And what about Reptar? Is it possible that he's forgiven the family who abandoned him in the first place? Who got the best deal out of this arrangement? Was it Reptar who had his life spared to be given one more chance, or was it each one of us who was given the opportunity to experience part of his life with him?

Things could have turned out different for Reptar had we given up on him. If the second foster family didn't give it their all, Reptar's life would've ended. If an experienced dog trainer didn't make room for Reptar and devote countless hours to rehabilitating him, Reptar wouldn't be with a family who loves him. That family would have been robbed of Reptar's love and devotion. If not for the first act of forgiveness and understanding and compassion, the love of a dog would have been cut short.

Maybe we can see this dog as a representation of us. Maybe Reptar symbolizes you and me and how we tend to lash out at people from time to time, even people we love and adore. We've all been injured and caused injury, and we've all been pardoned for it. Remember the partial quote I shared at the beginning of this chapter?" The one that started with, "Life's not the way it's supposed to be. It's the way it is…"? And then asked who said that? Here's the answer and the rest of the quote: It was said by the American sociologist, Virginia Satir, who is widely regarded as "the mother of family therapy." The other half of that quote is, "The way you cope with it is what makes the difference."

We all cope with life differently, it's not always the way it's supposed to be. But that doesn't mean we have to repay injury with more injury. Reptar was pardoned by a number of people, and he received a pardon unlike any you or I have ever thought of, he received a stay of execution. He was given a second chance.

It would seem to me that each one of us has been given a second chance at one time or another; in fact, I bet you can think of a name right now who's forgiven you for something you've done. We've both been pardoned, we've both bit the hand that feeds us and that same hand has eventually come back to take ours and share this journey with us. Perhaps that's the lesson, perhaps that's the Good News.

Reptar had Eiko and Rocky as accomplices in this
mission to destroy a roll of toilet paper.

Reptar sitting patiently waiting for a treat.

Dakota

… Where there is doubt, faith…

I'm an aviation junkie. I love the idea of flight and all the science that makes it possible. I blame this on my dad. As a young boy growing up in a small town, we learned to find wonder in all kinds of things, and one of them was planes that flew overhead. The Borough of Medford Lakes is a little more than one square mile. And up until a few years ago it only had one traffic light. Now it has two. It's probably as close as anyone could get to the feeling of growing up in Mayberry RFD. My brother, Glenn, and I were spoiled as kids, we just didn't realize it then.

Our community had (and still has) everything growing boys need—woods, fields, lakes, and one gas station. Nobody locked their doors and everybody knew one another. Streets were routinely closed for block parties and a tradition that goes back decades is still going on today, called "Canoe Carnival." Floats are built atop two canoes and they're paddled around the largest lake in the town on the first Saturday night in August.

And there's one church, the church where I served as youth minister until I got sick and had to take a medical leave of absence. It's a log cabin church, built more than sixty years ago. Beautiful stained glass windows let in just enough light to capture the authentic log craftsmanship that was the pride of the builders in that day. What it lacks in energy efficiency (the log walls on the inside are the same logs that make up the facade on the outside—no insulation) it more than makes up for in magnificence. Of all the things I miss by writing down here in south Florida, our church is at the top of the list.

Through the trees that make up the edge of the Pinelands National Reserve you could see commercial planes in their patterns going into two airports close to our home. Philadelphia

International Airport is a busy airport and we were lucky enough to have our home right under the pattern for planes that jockey for position to enter the final approach flight path. The other airport is a military post, McGuire Air Force Base. Those military cargo jets are *huge*! And they fly low so they don't interfere with the airspace of planes under the air traffic control of Philadelphia. And when we were growing up and every house had an antenna on its roof, we knew when every plane was flying overhead. If you're old enough to remember rabbit ears and directional rooftop TV antennas, you know what I'm talking about.

If we did hear a plane approaching, my dad would take my brother and me out back and he'd ask us to identify the type of aircraft. Was it a 737? Why did we think it was an L10-11? Was it the engine configuration or the tail that gave it away? Being an "airplane spotter" when he was in high school was his way of contributing to the war effort during World War II. A civilian network of airplane spotters helped scan the skies in an effort to thwart any surprise attacks. He joined the Army Air Corps when he graduated high school and would later share his love of airplanes with his two sons.

That was a long way of getting to this paragraph, I know. Sorry, I miss my dad. He died when I was in my early twenties. My mom died a year before him. They both loved animals and allowed me to have my own dog when I was nineteen, a Siberian Husky/Shepherd mix who I named "Niko." We had Teddy and Fluffy before Niko and I can't remember a time growing up when we didn't have a dog in the house.

Getting back to aviation, I love it so much that I spent thousands on helicopter lessons. I soloed and flew cross country, passed the written test in anticipation of my flight check, and was all ready to take it the following week. And then I was hospitalized with a possible heart attack. That took care of flying (and the expense that went along with it), but it didn't stop my love of aviation. So when the phone rang and I was told the next transport of foster dogs was coming in by airplane and the foster families would meet the dogs as they got out of the plane, I didn't even wait to be told what kind of dog we were getting. All I knew was that I was going to be able to hang around an airplane that just landed and maybe chat with the pilot. Count me in!

> No one appreciates the very special genius
> of your conversation as the dog does.
>
> —Christopher Morley

We weren't allowed to drive onto the runway to meet the plane, but we were permitted to walk up to the taxiway and wait. A planeload of dogs was onboard an incoming flight and all of us foster folks had our eyes trained to the sky in anticipation of more puppy kisses. After about twenty or thirty minutes (what seemed like an hour), I spotted a single engine plane on a downwind leg, abeam the numbers (of the runway). It was the only plane in the pattern and I knew it was *our plane*. I don't know why I knew it was our plane, we didn't have any communications with it and this was a small, private airport with no control tower. So I guess it would be more accurate to say I had a feeling, a strong feeling, that the plane I saw flying parallel to the airport setting up for a final approach was the plane we were all waiting for.

The plane turned onto the base leg and it looked like a Piper Arrow. Cool! From our vantage point on the apron, I was able to watch the plane bank and descend onto final approach. He had the numbers in sight and he was lined up perfectly. And his touchdown was just as nice. The pilot turned the plane around at the end of the runway and taxied to where we were standing. After he shut down the engine, he got out of the cockpit and greeted us with a look that said, "They're all yours!"

The pilot, Gary, from an organization called Pilots N Paws, had flown from Maryland with an airplane filled with crates of various sizes. And those crates contained dogs. After the crates were offloaded they were placed on the apron and that's when we got our first glimpse of Dakota. Dakota was a black dog, a Lab mix who didn't make eye contact with anyone who came near her. Black dogs are the most difficult to get adopted. Check out any shelter and you'll see more black dogs than any other color. The result is sad: Black dogs don't get adopted as easily as dogs of other colors, so they get euthanized more easily (and at a greater rate) than any other dog.

Even though Gary flew in from Maryland, that didn't mean that's where this transport of dogs came from. Pilots N Paws has more than 1,800 pilots volunteering their time. In order to get shelter dogs from one place to another, rescue organizations coordinate with the pilots to get dogs from shelters in distant states to their location. Sometimes dogs are shuttled from one plane to another during the transport, especially if there are a lot of miles (thousands) to travel. In essence, one pilot starts the first leg of the journey and meets another pilot at an airport at a midway point. Then that pilot loads the crates into his or plane and continues the second leg of the journey. And so on. And so on.

On this occasion, Gary loaded the crates into his plane from a pilot who flew into the airport in Maryland from a southern state where the dogs were in various shelters. A rescue organization in that state coordinated with our organization so we knew what dogs were coming and hopefully a little background on each one. Also involved with that coordinated effort were the folks at Pilots N Paws, and pilots like Gary. If you think the cost of gas is high for your car, imagine what the price is at a fuel pump at an airport! So many people, who sometimes literally fly under the cover of darkness, are involved in a transport like this. And most of them donate more than their time. This can get expensive.

And if you think your house can get a little stinky when your dog has an accident, think of what happens thousands of feet in the air, with nowhere to go but your destination that could be hours away. Accidents happen, and dogs coming from shelters are scared. They don't know what's going on. And they're in a crate, in a plane, for hours. Any guesses on what the first thing we did when we took hold of Dakota's leash? That's right, we found a grassy area and *let her go.* I mean "go," like going to the bathroom, not go like saying good-bye. Just in case you thought we let a dog loose on a runway...

Let me back up one step, back to the crate sitting on the airport apron with a scared and shivering black Lab mix cowering in the corner. Dakota was a beautiful looking dog—long, soft fur that felt like silk when you touched it. But it would be awhile before we'd be able to stroke it. And it would be a while before we could get her out of her crate. She wouldn't come near the door, maybe it was because of all the people crowded around, maybe it was a strange surrounding—the sights, the smells. Whatever it was, she wasn't coming out. I got a dog biscuit from another foster parent who was there to pick up her newest charge, this would surely work.

Nope. Not interested at all! The rest of the dogs were already in their new foster parent's cars, waiting to go to their new [temporary] home. We were standing on a pad of black asphalt looking at a crate with a black dog in it. We were down to one option: go in and get her. And once again, yours truly was "nominated" to do the dirty work. I think my background of being a canine handler was starting to work against me.

I knew Gary was on a schedule, a tight schedule, to get going. His window (the time frame pilots have to get to a certain place in order to avoid weather or meet certain flight rules) was closing quickly and he needed to get airborne soon. Another dog, another opportunity to crawl through a tight space to get to it. Where was Corey when I needed him? And don't forget, I would be eye level with a dog I never met, a dog that was scared to death and acting that way. When you crawl into a crate, there's not much room to turn around and get your face away from the working end of the animal that's staring at you. Well, at least we weren't committing another felony by this act. But I still would've suggested a younger, more able bodied, person take this on instead of a retired, disabled cop.

Since time wasn't on our side, I didn't have time to think. All I could do was look up at Elissa and say, "Wish me luck." Her reply, "You'll be fine, look how cute she is." Look, I don't know a lot about a lot, but I do know a little bit about a little, and one of the things I know is that not every dog that bites is ugly! Cute dogs have been known to bite from time to time. Enough talking, right? Time to go in.

I inched my way through the crate door and, on all fours, and made my way to within reaching distance of this terrified animal. Slowly I slipped the leash over her head until the loop of it was around her neck. And then I stopped. I couldn't help but look at this creature and wonder what had happened to her that made her this sad. I don't know how long I was kneeling there, but Elissa finally spoke up and told me to back out of the crate. Dakota still wouldn't look me in the eye, she kept her head turned away from me. I've been turned down by women before, lots of women, but this one hurt more than all of them combined!

As Elissa and the rest of the crew saw my best side inching back out of the crate toward them, I kept focused on the dog at the other end of the leash I was holding. I didn't want to turn my back on the girl who wouldn't even look at me. It reminded me of the high school dances I attended as a teenager. Only then I didn't have a leash to work with…

Every part of my body with the exception of my right hand cleared the crate door. I stopped again, hoping that if she didn't feel crowded in the crate, Dakota would feel safe with me and allow me to gently lead her by the leash out the door. Nope, not a chance. All that happened is that I looked stupid in my position on the pavement—a guy on all fours, barely able to move under the best of circumstances, trying to connect with a dog who had no intention of leaving her abode. However modest it was, Dakota seemed to think that the crate was her home and she wasn't moving.

Elissa helped me up and took the leash. I don't know what she said in dog language, but whatever it was, it worked. She was able to coax Dakota out of the crate and to her side. Dakota still didn't look at anyone and her tail was tucked between her legs, but at least she was out of the crate. That meant she could empty her bladder (and/or bowels) on the grassy area alongside the tarmac. And it meant Gary could get on his way. Everyone else left the airport with their new dogs and I came up with excuse after excuse to hang around to walk Dakota a little longer. By pure coincidence, Dakota appeared to me that she was ready to get in our car just as Gary's plane took off from Runway 19.

> Teach me how to trust my heart,
> my mind, my intuition, my inner knowing,
> the senses of my body.
> Teach me to trust these things so that I may
> enter my sacred space and love beyond
> my fear and thus walk in balance with
> the passing of each glorious sun.
>
> —Lakota Prayer

Dakota arrived home with us and we went through the routine of introducing her to the pack. No problems there; she was totally submissive and disinterested in any of the other dogs. We then let her run out back with the dogs. Everyone (the ones with four legs) couldn't wait to get out the door and romp in the yard. As soon as the door was cracked open a little bit, Eiko used his nose to nudge it open just enough to get his head in there and then, with his shoulders, he threw it wide open and all the dogs ran out.

All the dogs were running and playing, and peeing and pooping. All of them, except Dakota. She took herself to an area of the yard behind the shed and laid down. The rest of the pack ran up to her and tried to get her to play, but she wouldn't have any of it. We didn't know if she was sick. Could it be something serious? Was it more than just the long plane ride?

Elissa and I stood on the deck and watched. Helplessly, we observed a dog introduced to a pack that wanted to accept her, but she appeared to want no part of it. There was nothing we could do but watch from the railing of a deck that every other dog knew like the back of their hand—er, uh, paw. The deck served as a sort of staging area where dogs waited to come in and where they hung out and waited, if they were the first out, for the rest of the pack to assemble before racing to the grass in the backyard. It was safe, it offered comfort and reassurance. It's where we stood with our hearts breaking watching a dog become a loner instead of a member of a pack of animals that wanted to include her.

After a few minutes Elissa said she couldn't watch it anymore and went inside to make dinner (for the dogs). She called the dogs to go in with her and their internal clocks knew what that meant—dinnertime! They scrambled through the door, Bailey first and then the rest squeezed in behind her. Now it was just Dakota and me. I didn't know what to say; I didn't know what to do. More time passed as she wandered in a small arc, always using the shed as a barrier between herself and whatever was in the yard. In this case, me.

There was no trust, no bond of any sort that could be developed like this. Maybe if I showed her I wasn't there to hurt her, and she didn't come to us to be hurt. Maybe if I enticed one of her primal instincts: food. I went inside and grabbed a few biscuits out of the jar on the counter. Elissa looked at me like I was crazy. Before I could figure out why I got the look, I saw the dogs, who were all sitting at her feet, run toward me. And that's when it hit me, the dogs know where the biscuits are kept and they have the sound of the lid being removed committed to memory. I screwed up the whole dinner routine and Elissa would be stuck with resetting their attention and dealing with their disappointment in not getting a treat. As I was running back out the door, I looked back and said I was sorry.

Dakota wasn't even interested that I was gone, not a care or worry that the human was gone. When I came back out she was in the same place she was when I went in. I walked toward her, slowly so as not to spook her. She backed away. I avoided eye contact and acted like I was just taking a walk, not interested in her. She walked away some more. I held out my hand and got down on one knee. If I was holding a ring instead of a biscuit it would've looked like I was proposing. I thought of calling her to me. There was just one problem with that idea: she didn't have a name. From the first time we met her to this time of desperation, she was just the dog that we felt sorry for. We called her "poor baby" and "what a shame." But they weren't her names, they were feelings we had about her. They described the way we saw her. She arrived to us with no name and in the confusion and rush of getting her out of the crate, it never occurred to us to name her. And now she was in our backyard, afraid and lonely. Trusting no one. Not even a guy down on one knee offering a symbol of everlasting love—a dog biscuit.

"Hey, girl, come here, I have a treat for you." It was louder than a whisper but softer than a normal voice. "Here, girl, I got something for you." Nothing. Notta. Zilch. I went from one knee to two knees, now I looked like I was praying. And to be honest, I was. At least I tried. The question was who should I pray for? Should I pray for the dog in our yard, that she would find trust and come to me? Or should I pray for myself that I might discover some kind of wisdom and direction that would help me come up with the right words to get her to come to me?

Dinnertime had come and gone and the light was starting to fade. I stayed on my knees hoping for divine intervention. It never arrived. Ain't that a kick in the butt when you hope for the Divine to appear and you wait and you wait? And you wait some more. Again, nothing; notta, zilch. Doubt creeps in and before you know it, you lose hope. And if you're like me you might even get mad; disappointed again in the lack of His presence in your life. Have you ever just asked for a simple favor and got nothing for it? Yep, me too. Kinda sucks, doesn't it?

> Scratch a dog and you'll find a permanent job.
>
> —Franklin P. Jones

There's a finite time I can stay on my knees. Age and a rare disease doesn't give me much time down there, if I can get down there at all. And if I do manage to get on my knees, I need someone there to help me back up. Elissa was inside cleaning up and I didn't want to yell for her because the last time I yelled for her in the backyard she thought I really injured myself and came running out to save me. It turned out I just needed help getting out of the chair; I didn't need an ambulance, but she said I almost gave her a heart attack. All the windows were closed and I knew I would've had to yell really loud to get her attention. That might've given her another close call with the emergency medical services, so I chose not to ask for her help. Instead I sat back on my heels and just looked out into the yard.

Sitting on my heels, knees pushed onto the cold ground, I felt as helpless as ever. There was nothing more I could do than roll onto the ground. I mean, that's exactly all I could do; I couldn't get up and I didn't want to call Elissa for help. So I let gravity do its thing and leaned to the side and there I was, my left ear to the ground, with a view of our backyard that looked different than when viewed from the vertical position. I thought to myself I should've had Photoshop installed so I could rotate the picture ninety degrees.

But laying there gave me a perspective that I never even imagined before. It was probably the closest I ever got to see the world from the eyes of a dog. Especially a scared one with her head lowered. Everything looked bigger, taller to be exact. I decided I might as well just lie there; this decision after assuming all the dog poop had been cleaned up earlier in the day. God, I hope the kids picked it up…

I placed my elbow on the ground and propped the side of my head in my hand and took in the scenery. Perhaps if I looked like a male model in that pose Dakota would come to me? After all, who could resist a guy in my shape stretched out on his side wearing the latest fashion trends? After giving up on praying for wisdom and direction, after dismissing the idea that the Divine would intercede and grant Dakota trust, do you want to know what happened? She lifted her head up and looked at me. Her eyes met my eyes and she stopped, and for the first time since we met, she looked relaxed.

Maybe it *was* the pose I struck. Or maybe she met me at her own level. Whatever it was, it was working. And that meant I had a chance. All I needed now was some time to show her I wasn't a threat: no sudden moves, no more eye contact (that might signal I was challenging her), and definitely no loud noises. No sooner did those thoughts enter my brain than Elissa opened the back door and yelled out, "Rusty, where are you?" I looked back at Dakota (although not named that as of yet, it would become her name and it's easier for me to write than "that dog" right now) and saw that she was startled by this high school teacher's voice. Maybe like the kids in her classroom when they didn't have their homework done.

Dakota turned her back to me and put her head back down. Again I heard, "Rusty, where are you?" I didn't want to shout back and ruin all the progress we made, instead I tried whispering. I had my back to the house, so there wasn't much luck of her hearing me, but I figured I had nothing to lose. She didn't hear me. The next thing I heard was, "What the hell are you doing laying on the ground?" She'd found me, she walked out onto the deck and stood by the steps scanning the backyard for this hunk of a male model. When she saw the sight that could have shocked anyone, she cried out that rhetorical question. Actually, it was more than a rhetorical question, because more than once a family member found me in some sort of horizontal position, whether on the floor in one of the rooms in the house or in the yard. So I did at least understand her concern.

I tried waving her away with my free arm, silently shooing her away from me. Didn't work. "What are you doing?" was the next thing I heard. Only this time it was from directly above me. She had walked down the steps into the yard to see if I was okay. I was. But it was now too late for the connection between Dakota and me, she wandered off without so much as a good-bye. I was informed it had been almost a half an hour since she went in to feed the other dogs and she was getting worried. Especially when she looked out the kitchen window and couldn't find me. Elissa reminded me that it was getting dark and we couldn't leave this dog outside all night long, something had to give. I explained to her what had just happened between us and suggested that if she went inside, I might be able to get Dakota to come to me. She didn't have a jacket on, and neither did I. I hadn't planned for this to be a long process when I went out with the dog biscuits some thirty minutes earlier. I suggested that only one of us should risk freezing to death and since chivalry wasn't dead in our house, I elected myself to be the one to continue shivering. Elissa gladly agreed with my suggestion and ran back into the house with her arms crossed in front of her, hands grabbing opposite shoulders, mumbling what sounded like "brrr" under her breath.

It was back to just the two of us. Was she spooked, did we scare her away and I'd have to wait another thirty minutes for her to trust me again? Thankfully, that answer came relatively quickly. Minutes after Elissa went inside to get warm, Dakota reappeared from behind the shed. But instead of staying where she was before Elissa came out, Dakota continued moving toward me. And not in an unsure way. She held her head up, her tail was hanging normally and not tucked up between her legs, her ears were up. And she didn't take her eyes off of me. Man, I hope she didn't all of a sudden feel hungry and see me as an easy meal!

There was nothing I could do if she did see me as human dog food, I was on the ground and I would stay there until someone in the house came out to help me up. This is where, for Dakota and me, doubt turned to faith. We trusted each other. Without saying a word, we knew what the other was (and wasn't) thinking. Dakota walked right up and sat down in front of me. Then she did something amazing: she gave me her paw. There, freezing my rear end off on a lump of cold, damp grass, I witnessed something magnificent. Sure, a dog giving someone her paw isn't exactly newsworthy, but this was more than any dog giving any person a paw. This was, before this moment in time, a terrified creature who didn't know what was going on in her world. This moment was about trust. And faith. All I could do was look up and say, "Thank you."

I wanted to share this moment with everyone, but no one was there to see it. I wanted my family to experience what I just experienced, but it was just Dakota and me. I wanted it to last. So I grabbed her paw lightly. She apparently wanted more. I got a swat from her that she wanted something more than a handshake. She pawed at my hand, pushing it down, away from her arm. My fingers landed right against her chest. That was it, this girl was smart!

For the next couple of minutes I scratched her chest and belly, but mainly her chest. She seemed to enjoy it there the most. I ran my hand up under her chin a couple of times, just like the dog behavioral specialists suggest when meeting a new dog for the first time. But each time I scratched under her chin I got the paw. It was as if she was telling me to get busy somewhere else on her body, and the look in her eyes when I reached her chest told me that was the spot.

I took this opportunity to take our relationship to the next level, but like on any first date, a guy really never knows if he's moving too fast. Inside my pants pocket was the handful of dog biscuits I had grabbed earlier. Now if I could just get them out of my pocket. I would need both arms for this: one to hold me up off the ground and the other to reach in and grab them. In order to give her what I thought she wanted I would first have to stop doing something I knew she liked. Yeah, you tell me if this didn't sound *exactly* like a first date. Or second. Or third. Or marriage...

Wait, how'd that get in there?

It's true, though, isn't it? We're never really quite sure if we should give up something we know is working in order to risk that which might take us to the next level—in relationships, in careers, in life. I found this to be the case as I was looking up at a dog who appeared to be content with me petting her—the rest of the night. I rolled to one side and before I could reach in with my free hand I got the paw. I tried rolling the other way, using the other arm. Same result. I was afraid if I stopped she would wander to the back of the yard and we'd have to start over. And by this time my body had begun to absorb the cold and damp of the ground. So I contorted my body in a way that had me reaching straight out with the hand that was scratching and twisting onto my hip so I could squeeze my free hand into my pocket. And of course, the biscuits were in that part of the pocket that was still under my body.

Eventually I was able to retrieve a treat and offer it to Dakota. It would be my second sign of affection and although it wasn't flowers like most girls would want on a date, I was betting that this girl was different than the rest I ended up on the ground with (in my much younger days) and she'd appreciate the gesture. And sure enough, she did. Hesitant at first to take it, she accepted my offer and seemed to enjoy it. I told her that if she liked that, she would love Elissa's cooking. I knew she'd been traveling all day and she had to be famished. So I got up to my knees, rolling onto my stomach and then pushing up and rolling back over into a seated position. I was afraid that I might startle her, but she stayed right there in front of me. The second dog biscuit was easier to get to than the first and she took this one right away. I was making progress. We were bonding. She was beginning to trust me more and more with each passing minute. I sat there and fed her biscuit after biscuit until there was only one left, not because I thought this was the right way to feed a hungry dog, but because I had no choice. I was stuck there until Elissa came out to help me up. And the last biscuit would be used as an "emergency treat" if the need arose—that is, if Elissa coming outside scared Dakota and she ran off.

Lucky for both us, Elissa's concern for me is both constant and tenacious. I don't get away with much and when I do get away with something I'm not supposed to be doing, it usually comes back to bite me in the behind and I end up explaining to her what I did anyway. No sooner had I run out of biscuits (like a guy running out of things to say on a blind date) when Elissa came back outside. This time there was no yelling, no wondering where I was. She knew I'd be in the same spot she left me. She walked over to us slowly, and asked how it was going. I told her me and my date were now getting along great, but it was time for both of us to go inside. Elissa helped me up to my feet and there, in the last minutes of daylight, Elissa gave her the name, Dakota.

Elissa said this dog reminded her of a Native American who'd been displaced by no fault of her own. While she was inside feeding the other dogs and cleaning up after them, she thought of this dog and her travels and decided a Native American name would best suit her. And she named her Dakota. We would later learn that this name meant "friend" or "ally."

Know yourself. Don't accept your dog's admiration as
conclusive evidence that you are wonderful.

—Ann Landers

I used the last biscuit to persuade Dakota to follow me inside by holding it in my closed hand and coaxing her to follow me. One thing we didn't count on was the welcoming committee waiting just inside the back door. Would Dakota see them, get overwhelmed, and run away, or would she see the noses pressed against the glass as friends and allies? Can you imagine being in her shoes? You're hungry, you're cold, you're scared, and a bunch of folks you never met before are clamoring to see you. Are you a starlet or a threat? For me, I saw my first date with Dakota as a success and I wanted to keep it going. So Elissa went in first and corralled them in the living room. My date and I then entered the back door together and her reward for trusting me was the last biscuit; she took it gently from my cold hand. But now she had to find a way to assimilate with the pack. Truth time.

Bailey was let out of the living room first. Some butt sniffing on her part was the thumbs-up the rest of the pack needed and before long the rest of the dogs were in the kitchen introducing themselves (more—a lot more—butt sniffing) like a classroom would be to a new student. Slowly, Dakota's tail rose to where it was being held high in the air and instead of being the one chased, she chased a few pack members in a playful way of telling them she could hold her own.

Now, some three hours after she arrived by plane, Dakota was part of our pack. And to show her just how much she was welcomed in the home, Elissa did what she does best at doggie-dinnertime—she cooked some chicken and added it to a bowl of dog food and gave it to Dakota. The rest of the pack was kept out of the room as Dakota enjoyed fine dining in a private dining room. It was just her and me, me and her; our date was continuing well past, if history serves me correctly, a point most of my other dates in life didn't reach. Elissa gave us our time together and it was nice to see Dakota relaxed and enjoying a meal. Maybe her first meal in a home ever. Sad when you think of it that way. But we had bonded and there was nothing that could come between us now.

Until she was done eating. That's when she left the kitchen to retire to the living room where the others were waiting. Once she got there and saw how they played, she never looked back at me. She was a dog and they were her equals. I felt bad, but I felt good, if that makes sense. Seeing a dog get along with every member of the pack is a sight that makes you smile. You just want her to be happy. Like seeing my date at the sophomore dance go home with the school's star quarterback—she was happy and that's what was important...

Let's not overplay the date analogy, I'm over it more than three decades later. But you know what I'm still not over? All the work I put into getting her to trust me, to trust a human, and who do you think she curls up with when the playing in the living room stopped? If you guessed Elissa sitting in her comfy chair, you'd be right! It's a sight to see the energy slowly leave the room as each dog tires out from playing. They all find a spot to claim as theirs once they're too pooped to play any longer. Some head for the sofa, maybe the love seat; one dog might even come up with the crazy idea of their own to lie down on the floor—you know, on a dog bed that's made for them—not a piece of furniture that's made for a human.

Once all the spots were claimed, Dakota looked around and I moved to the side of my chair to make room for her. After all, she'd want to come sit with me so I could pick up where I left off in the yard—scratching her chest until my arm was tired. All she had to do was climb up and I'd show her how we love dogs in the Williams Canine Hotel.

She walked right past me. Right past me to Elissa, *who wasn't even looking in her direction.* She put one paw on the chair, then the other. She looked at Elissa who had her laptop opened and Elissa looked back at her. The laptop was closed, Elissa's butt shifted over and the next thing I know I'm looking at Dakota sharing a chair with Elissa. What about the time we spent in the yard? What about the biscuits I fed you? What about the moments we shared?

After that first night, Dakota followed Elissa everywhere. She was the first to line up in the hallway every afternoon to wait for Elissa to get home from work, and she was the first to climb in bed with her at night. In no time at all Dakota found a human she could trust and love. A human who trusted and loved her back. And me? I was always her second choice. When Elissa was at work, Dakota snuggled with me. If Elissa was out shopping, Dakota played with me. But when Elissa was home, forget it. Maybe it was the chicken dinners?

It shouldn't have been about us, should it? Dakota was a dog and the greatest joy both Elissa and I got was watching her play with the other dogs in the yard. The way she ran made her coat look like it was flowing in the wind behind her. She ran with a stride that was both effortless and elegant. She reminded everyone who saw her of a free spirit. And they thought the name, Dakota, fit her perfectly.

Dakota was adopted by a young couple one town away from us. Saying good-bye was tough, one of the hardest up until that time. But we knew she was going to a good home, and our job was never to be her forever home. We were a stayover point in Dakota's life, a place where she would learn how to be a dog with other dogs and how to socialize with humans. It was a leap of faith on both sides.

> I think life is like a good book. The further you
> get into it, the more it begins to make sense.
>
> —Harold Kushner

What would've happened if Dakota never warmed up to me? How would her life have turned out if she finally didn't trust me enough to come over to me and give me her paw? If Elissa and I didn't invest countless hours of helping her come out of her shell, would she have been adopted?

Sometimes in life we have to work hard at developing trust, other times it just happens. Look at me and Dakota and Elissa and Dakota: I had to work hard, Elissa just let it happen. When we think of faith, do we ever consider that there'll be hard work ahead? Someone much wiser than me once said, "Faith without works is dead." And while I doubt the reputed author (James) was thinking about fostering dogs when he was credited with this much used quote (maybe used too much in the wrong context, but that's a sermon for another book), the concept of those words has a way of reminding us that our work is never done.

We can have all the faith in the world in something, but if we don't get off our butts and do something (like reaching into your pocket for a dog biscuit), the very thing we have faith in might just stand there and look at us. And then what? How fulfilling would our lives feel like if all we did was lie on a cold ground and wait? It took more than thirty minutes of pleading, coaxing, and calling for a shy dog to even come near me. I can't imagine what either of our lives would be like right now if Elissa and I had just given up or left her be outside.

Think for a moment the faith Dakota had. Her head had to be filled with emotions like confusion, fear, sadness, loneliness, and maybe even anger. Something inside of her had to motivate her to take that first step. It was Martin Luther King Jr. who said, "Take the first step in faith. You don't need to see the whole staircase, just take the first step."

For me, the Good News here is that doubt doesn't have to be our driving force. With a little bit of work, sometimes *a lot* of work, we can indeed replace doubt with faith. We can see faith in others instead of doubting their motives; we can see faith in our works instead of doubting our skills; we can *have* faith in others and we can *have* faith in ourselves.

Maybe Dakota can remind all of us that unnamed things in our lives can have a purpose, a purpose that, at the time, is unclear to us. She can remind us that perseverance and determination can put faith back in relationships—relationships that have names like mom or dad, daughter or son, brother or sister, aunt or uncle, niece or nephew, sister or brother. Nameless relationships oftentimes become our most precious memories—once we put a name to them.

And when we might have doubts, let's not forget this when we think of perseverance and determination: These two human character traits can be part of the naming of a cherished relationship, namely "friend" or "ally."

Dakota guarding the channel changer.

The dogs are lined up waiting for Elissa to come home from work. They did this every day at the same time.

Bear and Shadow

...Where there is despair, hope...

Sometimes the names just come to you. After more than a few *successful* foster adoptions from our home, Taryn became more comfortable with letting us name the dogs that would be in our care. Remember, there is a real danger in naming the dog yourself, the emotional attachment dramatically increases the risk of you becoming a foster failure, of you adopting the dog yourself. Every rescue organization has volunteer homes filled with dogs that were brought in to be fostered, but ended up staying in that foster home forever. On the positive side, most rescue organizations wave the adoption fee when that happens!

But this isn't about whether or not we'd be failures or success stories, this is about two Lab mixes that arrived one afternoon. They were brother and sister and they, along with two other brothers and their pregnant momma, were transported up from another southern state where the euthanasia rate in shelters is extremely high. Not only was this litter of dogs less than a year old going to be killed, so was their pregnant mother. Yes, you read that right: these siblings were less than a year old and their mother was pregnant again. Puppy mills don't just breed purebred dogs, and the back story here is that whoever "owned" the mother didn't want to care for her anymore. Since none of her puppies (the ones in this transport) had been bought, they were thought of as expendable as well. It's amazing what we, as a society, can become when we no longer believe something—even a *living thing*—has value.

These puppies didn't sell, and the owner probably thought the still-to-be-born puppies inside this momma weren't going to fare any better. So why not dispose of them all? Get a fresh start, clean the slate and start over with a new dog, maybe one that has "cuter" offspring...

Yep, I get downright pissed off when I start to think of what happens to living creatures who can't fend for themselves and, for reasons that are beyond their control, they die. They die because they are killed. We can put a sterile, official-sounding medical term to it like *euthanize*, but the result is the same: these animals are killed. Sickening is as close as I can come to describing this feeling.

But for every person who has such a disregard for the value of life, we come across ten more who do value life. Maybe the percentages are even higher than that; I bet less than ten percent of the people we encounter are inherently bad. I'll take those odds. And I'll focus on the good in people. Who's in this with me?

Are we suckers for trying to see the good in people? For continuously searching for high morals and true values while overlooking the faults that every one of us has? I guess I—*we*—could be called far worse things for worse reasons. I'm also a sucker for anything that demonstrates honor or valor. I can't hear "Taps" played on a bugle without tearing up, I've attended too many police officer's funerals. Same with "Amazing Grace" on the bagpipes, for the same reason, I become a blubbering idiot as soon as that first note is hit. I've also been called a sucker (among other things) for trusting too easily and forgiving too freely. Again, there are worse things a person can be called.

But what about a dog? What things do we call a dog when he or she is too trusting or too forgiving? Do we think they're naïve for trusting us? Do we see them as idiots for forgiving us like they do? Any chance they feel foolish when they're deceived by one of us human creatures who share the earth with them?

> Animals share with us the privilege of having a soul.
>
> —Pythagoras

I hope that if dogs do indeed truly forgive, Bear and Shadow forgive me for the two easy puns made after we named them. Shadow was a dog that looked like a Lab mix, a pitch black coat, longer than that of a Lab, but nonetheless, easily identifiable as being at least part Lab. Her personality was as sweet as any dog that came through our door. And her eyes—her eyes seemed to be able to look at you in a way that had you melting in no time. To a person, everyone who met Shadow remarked at how she looked at them—the beauty in her eyes. Her eyes always followed you, like a shadow. And so, she was named Shadow.

Bear was a large dog, in fact he was larger than Eiko. Bear's eyes were sunken, almost sad. His coat was thick and wavy, with colors of auburn and an orange tone to it that contrasted to the black underlying color. His paws were huge. Bear's ears stood straight up, not floppy like you'd expect to see in a Lab, they were triangular shaped and they stood up on his head all the time. He reminded us of the *Muppet* character Fozzie Bear. And because of that we named him Bear.

The puns seemed to write themselves, first Shadow and then Bear. Beside her eyes following everyone like a shadow does, I thought it would be great to tell everyone that I love "seeing my Shadow." Lame, huh? Okay, maybe you'll understand my pleasure in choosing to give Bear his name. Our backyard is wooded toward the rear of it and I can't tell you how much I loved proving an age-old question: A Bear really does "do that" in the woods. Was that second one better? Look, it's the little things in life that make me smile.

The first night in our house involved all the normalcies we'd become accustomed to. But their baths were different. They were different not because we changed our routine (no way, we were pros by now), but because of what we found during the baths. Let's retrace to the beginning when we picked them up. As with most transports, the dogs arrive dirty; some arrive downright filthy. They all get bathed regardless of how they look (and feel), but when you see the grime and bugs on some of them, you know the bath is a priority when you get them home.

When they arrived as a family of a momma and her four offspring, none of us knew what we were getting. Elissa and I had agreed to take two of the dogs, two other foster families were each taking one of the litter, and another family had agreed to take the pregnant momma. Since we were the first to arrive when the three crates were unloaded, we were given the choice of which dogs we wanted to bring home. The momma was in one crate and the two other crates each had two siblings. For reasons that still aren't clear to me, we chose a crate that was holding Bear and Shadow.

We took them out of the crates and hooked them up to our own leashes. Then they were microchipped and given a quick wipe down with a bunch of those dog wipes because they stunk. They stank, they reeked; they really stunk of an odor that none of us ever smelled before. And it was as we were wiping them down that we found what looked like huge ticks on the dogs. Bear and Shadow seemed to have the most of them. We figured we wouldn't try to remove them until we got them home and gave them baths so we could really see what we were dealing with. Once they were cleaned thoroughly at our house, we set about the task of removing those weird looking ticks. There was just one problem: they weren't ticks!

Once their fur was pulled away, we could see that what we thought were ticks were actually growths on their skin. Some were small and some were really big, big and ugly like heads of cauliflower attached to different body parts. Shadow had maybe eight or ten, Bear had dozens. And his were oozing blood. They looked more than uncomfortable, they looked painful. After recognizing that they weren't ticks, it became obvious that we didn't recognize them as anything we'd ever seen before.

It's times like these that you're grateful you have a relationship with your veterinarian where you've exchanged cell phone numbers. Dr. Lori Cobb is our personal vet and she and her staff have proven time and again that they're compassionate beyond what's expected. And because of that I was able to take some pictures of these growths and send them to Dr. Cobb. Without seeing Bear and Shadow in the office, Dr. Cobb wasn't able to give a definitive diagnosis based solely on the pictures, but she did alleviate our concerns that Bear and Shadow would be okay until they could be seen by our rescue organization's primary veterinary office. Dr. Cobb suggested that the growths appeared to be caused by the papilloma virus.

The papilloma virus in dogs is relatively benign, unless it interferes with eating or the respiratory tract. This is what we learned after doing extensive research the rest of the night; searching the internet and reading every blog we could, reading every article we could find, and looking over dozens of images of the virus. Everything we read and images we reviewed seemed to confirm what Dr. Cobb told us; the pictures on the internet sites were almost identical to what we saw on Bear and Shadow. We also learned that there is no cure for this virus, it's treated *symptomatically*—that is, the symptoms are treated to relieve discomfort, but the only treatment to get rid of these growths is time. The rescue organization's primary veterinarian would have to be contacted and appointments made for Bear and Shadow to be seen and get full examinations.

> Personally, I would not give a fig for
> any man's religion whose horse,
> cat and dog do not feel its benefits.
> Life in any form is our perpetual responsibility.
>
> —S. Parkes Cadman

Different rescue organizations have different rules about how each foster dog is treated in the foster home. Some organizations ask their foster families to keep the foster dogs separate from their family—both human and canine family members. Other organizations ask their foster families to have strict rules about the dogs they're fostering, such as not letting dogs on their furniture and not allowing them to sleep in bed with them. These rules are put into place by rescue organizations for a number of reasons: safety is first and second is being able to keep a state of detachment so adoption is easier (less risk of being a foster failure). Another reason that needs to be mentioned is that when the dog does get adopted, you don't want it to get into trouble as soon as it gets to its forever home because it jumped on the couch or tried to sleep with its new owners.

Elissa and I have heard these rules, and more, from people we've met who were volunteering with other rescue organizations. We listened to all of them and after processing what we knew and what we were told, we decided—with the blessings of Taryn—to come up with our own rules. They were as follows:

Rule #1: Each foster dog that comes into our home will be treated just like any other canine family member.

Rule #2: Rule #1 shall be enforced at all times.

That's it. Plain and simple. We saw it analogous to being a foster home for children. If we had children of our own and we decided to foster another child, how would we treat him or her? We knew we wouldn't make that child eat at different times than our family. And we knew we wouldn't disallow that child to share in activities that our own children enjoyed. We simply couldn't imagine making that child feel different than the other children in our home. And we would hold our own children accountable for their behavior and we'd expect them to treat this new member of our household as one of their own family.

We would also make sure we held ourselves accountable. We decided we wouldn't shield any foster dog that came into our home from anyone who decided to visit us. All of our friends and family knew what we'd gotten ourselves into and they also knew what to expect when they walked through our front door. Our hope was that the foster dogs would get used to different people coming and going. When you have two children in college, there is a lot of coming and going with their friends alone. These new dogs came from shelters where they might not have been exposed to humans other than being fed or having their cage cleaned. We knew they needed to be exposed to as many different situations as possible if they were to feel comfortable around people other than us.

They needed to be socialized if they were to have any chance of being adopted.

Now this was definitely a double-edged sword. Giving puppies freedom can produce interesting results, and it usually does! We never left puppies alone in the home when we were gone. All of them were crate trained. This not only kept them safe while we were gone, it greatly increased the odds of our home looking the same when we returned as when we left. But when we were home, the dogs were able to be dogs. And our home doesn't look the same because of it.

But every chewed piece of woodwork has a name to it, a memory that will last long after we replace and repaint it. Every stain on the floor has a story to it and we'll laugh at them whenever we think of the dog who left us that calling card. Each piece of dog hair, all of them, embedded in our furniture serves to remind us of a love shared—a love shared not only with Elissa and me, but a love shared with our own dogs as well. There is something really special between dogs who share a love that says, "Here, you lie on the sofa tonight."

Yes, our friends think we're nuts. Some of our extended family members can't believe what we allow. And a few friends with other rescue organizations admonish us for screwing up dogs that come into our care. I'd agree with the first two statements—we are nuts and maybe we should have our heads examined. But screwing up the dogs? Neither Elissa nor I can imagine *love* screwing up a living creature.

Three dogs can be fun. Four dogs in the home, and things get really interesting. Five dogs make feeding time challenging. Any more than five dogs and things can get out of control in a hurry. So you can imagine what was going through our heads when we said yes to taking in Bear and Shadow—we already had five dogs in the house! But what were we supposed to do? What do you say when you're told if these dogs aren't pulled from the shelter they'll be put down in less than forty-eight hours?

We said, "What's two more mouths to feed?" When Bear and Shadow arrived, we had seven dogs in our home along with two cats. Cats and dogs who didn't know each other, dogs of different ages and various backgrounds, all with behaviors and temperaments that kept us up on more than a few nights. And speaking of nights, do you know what it's like to try to sleep with that many dogs… in your bed? A queen-size bed is what we have, two king-size beds are what we need!

> Surround yourself with dreamers and doers, the believers and the thinkers, but most of all surround yourself with those who see greatness within you, even when you don't see it yourself.
>
> —Edmund Lee

Bear and Shadow were now members of our family and regardless of their skin conditions, they would be allowed wherever the rest of the pack was permitted. So that first night they were welcomed up to our bedroom when it was time for bed. They had crates with blankets in them in the family room, but we made sure to invite them up to bed. Not knowing their background made helping them adjust a little harder, but we never imagined they wouldn't want to come to bed with us. As each light was turned off making the first floor a little darker with each flick of the switch, Bear and Shadow stayed by their crates. We always leave on a dimmed light and that's how we left them that first night.

As the rest of the pack got settled in, and we took turns brushing our teeth, Bear and Shadow stayed downstairs. When we peeked over the balcony that overlooks the family room, we saw that they were in their crates. We didn't know whether to be sad or feel relief that instead of fighting seven dogs for a spot in the bed, we'd only have to contend with five.

I tossed and turned all night worried about Bear and Shadow. We'd fostered a bunch of dogs by this point and every one of them wanted to sleep with the rest of the pack in our bed. I was worried something was wrong; like a first-time father always running in and checking his child in the nursery, I kept getting up and checking on Bear and Shadow. And like most first-time fathers, I finally realized that they were all right.

In the morning we saw that Shadow had been busy during the night; she took all the pillows off the sofas and brought them into her crate. Every pillow in the first floor was in her crate. I don't know what kind of furniture or decorating you like, but I'm married to a woman who believes there should be multiple pillows on every available piece of furniture. Don't even get me started with what our bed looks like every night before we get in it. I don't get it: If you're only going to sleep on one pillow—a pillow that's made to be slept on—why do you need ten more piled up on the *real* pillows? Apparently it looks nice. So I've been told.

Just as nice looking was the sight of seeing Shadow surrounded by all those pillows. Why do you think she gathered them up during the night? Did they give her security? Could she have liked the way they smelled? After all, I've been told that dogs gather (*and chew*) things in the house that have the scent of their owners on them. Maybe she was just bored. Whatever the reason, it was darn cute to see that first thing in the morning. Bear, on the other hand, not so cute. He looked like a sad-sack, he lifted his head and wagged his tail, but that was it.

This rescue organization is lucky enough to have a relationship with a veterinarian like we have with Dr. Cobb. By midmorning we had an appointment with Dr. Keefe, a vet who's helped so many dogs brought into foster care that he knows a lot of us foster families by name. Dr. Keefe confirmed what Dr. Cobb suspected. He removed one wart from each dog and sent them off to pathology, just to be certain. But there was another reason to lance one growth off of each dog: the papilloma virus is fought off by the body's immune system, and a lot of times when one growth is removed the immune system is sent into a kind of overdrive that starts fighting this menacing virus. These growths had deep roots and there was a hole left in the skin where each was removed. A few staples closed the holes and we left with a round of antibiotics for Bear and Shadow that would also help.

Days turned into weeks, and there was no change. In fact, we thought we saw new growths on both dogs. Shadow had one forming on her lip. Bear's were bleeding more and we found one in the pad of his front paw. No wonder he seemed sad, no wonder he didn't want to play and romp with the other dogs. Elissa started doing more research on this and she found supplements that would help boost their immune systems. But this was now at a time where I was going to be in the hospital for a little while and Bear and Shadow were going to another home, temporarily, until I was back home and on the mend. Selfishly, our focus had turned to me and my upcoming surgery and away from Bear and Shadow.

Mary, another foster in our organization, took Bear and Shadow for us. It was reassuring to know we could count on someone to help us out when our attention was needed elsewhere. This is one of the wonders of rescue organizations—everyone pitches in when needed. I think you'd agree that this kind of compassion and selflessness demonstrates that us foster folks aren't just a bunch of crazy animal lovers who put the needs of pets above our own. Mary demonstrated what happens every day in rescues all across the country: People who are involved with a cause greater than their own tend to jump in and lend a hand wherever it's needed—be it a human need or an animal need.

While Mary had Shadow and Bear, she made arrangements with another veterinarian to examine Bear as his growths seemed to be multiplying every day. This doctor felt that Bear's discomfort would get worse if the growths weren't removed, and while it wouldn't be a simple surgery, this doctor felt Bear would do well. It took not only this vet, but another one helping him, hours to remove most of the growths that were causing Bear so much discomfort. The surgery was extensive, but Bear recovered nicely and just about the time I got back on my feet from my visit to the hospital, Bear and Shadow came back to us.

You'd think that orders to do nothing for eight weeks would mean having a bunch of dogs around was a bad thing. But I really think that it helped me recuperate quicker than I would have in a house with no canine companionship. As I slowly regained strength, so did Bear. And Shadow was turning into a real love-bug, even though her growths were still visible.

Now with all of our collective medical procedures behind us, Elissa and I went back in research mode to see more about the supplements that boost the immune systems in dogs. We found a company that sold a powdered product that was added to food. We ran it by our vet, Dr. Cobb, and she was able to research the ingredients in the supplement and believed at the worst it wouldn't harm Bear and Shadow and at best, it would help them fight off the virus.

A few dollars later we had the product at our doorstep and began the regiment suggested in the packaging. To be honest, we were hopeful but not confident that this would help. It was simple enough to administer, just sprinkle it into their food bowls twice a day; the hard part was remembering to do it. We didn't expect anything the first week or so, we figured the supplement would take some time building up in their immune systems.

Two weeks, still nothing. Three weeks, notta. But about a month after we started them on the supplement, we noticed Shadow's growths shrinking. The few that were left on Bear dried up and fell off. Shadow's growths took a little while to fall off, but eventually she was clear of all her growths as well. The transformation we witnessed in both dogs was nothing short of amazing.

Bear not only recovered nicely from his surgery, but he recovered from the sadness that arrived with him months earlier. He was more alert, and more willing to take risks when people came over for a visit. When the growths were all over his body, he'd stay in his crate and very rarely interact with strangers. While Shadow and the rest of the pack were busy greeting visitors at our front door, Bear stayed back and watched from a distance.

But now that the growths were removed, he played with the other dogs. He even began instigating tug-of-wars in the backyard with whatever stick was handy. Watching Bear romp with the others dogs was one of the most rewarding things Elissa and I witnessed during our time fostering him and his sister. And being a witness to Shadow developing into a sweet dog who desperately wanted to please others made our hearts melt. And even though she wasn't as reserved as Bear when she still had those ugly warts on her, she came out of her shell in a way that made everyone who met her take notice.

The supplement seemed to work so well on Bear and Shadow that we decided to add it to everyone's food. We figured a boost in the immunity systems of dogs had to have benefits that we didn't fully understand, and it turned out we were right. The coats of the other dogs became softer and their eyes seemed to light up even more than before. In the end, it proved to be a good decision.

As anyone who goes into dog rescue knows,
it is not a for-profit business,
but the rewards are priceless for me.

—Emmylou Harris

Bear and Shadow were the first foster dogs we had that required medical care. Maybe up until that point we'd been lucky. As mentioned earlier, our organization is extremely fortunate to have a relationship with a vet who can be called anytime, day or night. And Dr. Keefe makes room in his day for emergencies that arise. You can imagine if a rescue organization has twenty or so foster homes, there is a constant risk of at least one of those homes having a medical issue. Elissa and I also feel fortunate for the relationship we developed with our personal vet, Dr. Cobb. It certainly gives us a level of comfort to know there is no question or concern too small that she won't answer as soon as she's able. We're never made to feel foolish if the concern is a false alarm and we had nothing to worry about all along. And both Dr. Keefe and Dr. Cobb share a level of compassion that is unmatched. That compassion carries over to financial compassion as well. Any doctor deserves to be compensated for their time; these doctors give their time to worthwhile groups like ours and without their understanding of financial constraints, it would be hard to continue.

Two years ago I was brought onto the board of directors for our organization. In that capacity I get to see the bills. The only source of income for this nonprofit rescue is through donations. Whenever a dog comes into our rescue in need of medical care, people from all over donate to the cause. And since we made a decision to pull dogs with medical conditions (dogs that would surely be euthanized due to their illness), our bills have skyrocketed. The surgery for Bear was higher than any procedure for any dog up to that date. Thousands were needed to cover the cost, and that cost was cut dramatically by the doctors who performed the operation. Their compassion can also not be overstated.

We had bills to pay and we were now looking at an invoice that would put us in the red. What's an organization to do? We hit social media and the result was immediate. Pictures of Bear went up on Facebook and other sites and before too long we had donations pouring in. Why does the picture of a suffering dog evoke so many emotions in us humans? As a cop I responded to thousands of calls over my twenty-five-year career, and some were gruesome. And during my four years as a paramedic before that I saw way too much suffering, so much so that I still have night terrors that wake up the entire family. I learned to deal with all that crap. I guess I found a way to compartmentalize everything so I don't have to deal with it. How about you? What do you do when you witness or experience something that's so horrible you can't believe it actually happened?

I bet you and me are a lot alike. And if you are, you might find the image of a suffering animal almost harder to deal with than human suffering. I don't share that in hopes of you seeing me as callous and hardened so much that I care more about animals than I do about humans. I don't. But there's something about seeing an animal suffering, hurting in ways that we really can't understand because they can't tell us, that brings me to tears. Maybe that's why requests for donations to help an animal are so successful. Whatever their reasons, people seem to reach deep into their pockets to help a living creature that's in pain.

That was the case with Bear. And thanks to the generosity of people we would never meet, the books were balanced and the doctors were paid. But none of that would have been possible if not for the kindness of humans—humans who show compassion and mercy. The news is filled with people who do horrible things, wouldn't it be nice if every now and then we heard stories of how strangers help people they don't even know?

Maybe that's the lesson here. Maybe all we need is the story of a helpless animal in need to stir our emotions to the point where we want to help. The stories of rescue organizations and how they got their start, stories of families coming together to foster dogs that are about to be discarded, stories of doctors who demonstrate their love for all of God's creatures, stories of individuals who step up and give a hand when one is needed. These stories need to be shared. In doing so we share the idea that love is a verb, it's not a noun.

We were surprised that Bear was adopted before Shadow. Shadow was so outgoing and lively we thought for sure she'd get adopted as soon as all those nasty growths were gone. But a family came to our home after seeing Bear on one of the pet adoption sites where we post pictures and short bios of every dog in our foster homes. They were looking for a laidback dog and Bear fit their mental image of what they had in mind. Driving Bear to their home after they completed the application and background check was hard. Other than driving back and forth to doctor's appointments, Bear hadn't been in a car. What was he thinking? Did he think he was going to get more stuff done to him by one of those people with a stethoscope around their neck?

Thankfully, he did great. In fact, as soon as we got out of the car Bear went right to the front door. We parked in the street, between the family's house and one of their neighbor's. There was no way Bear could have known where to go, let alone to the correct front door. It was as if he knew where he was supposed to go and as sad as it was to see him go, the joy we felt watching him run around the first floor of his new home caused us to laugh. His new family knew how to handle dogs and he was in the right place. We said our good-byes and walked out to the car silent; Corey came with us for moral support and it was needed. Elissa and I shared memories of Bear through tears the entire way back home. We were both thankful for being able to witness what we just did, but also that Corey was willing to take the driving responsibilities.

Shadow stayed with us for months after Bear was adopted. She went to a home with a dog named Jerry—the family who adopted Shadow enjoys the music from The Grateful Dead. This young couple was just what Shadow needed, a family where she could be herself and they, in return, would give her the love she deserved. The wife of this couple was pregnant when they first met Shadow and since then she has given birth to a baby boy. We still keep in touch via Facebook and the pictures of Shadow and Jerry are like a breath of fresh air. As are the pictures of Shadow with their precious little boy.

If Bear and Shadow could talk, I wonder if they'd tell us they had any hope in them when they arrived in our home. Covered in grime and thrust into a new home, given multiple baths by people they didn't know; only to find out they had a virus that would cause pain and misery for months to come. What would they tell us of their journey to being adopted? Where did the idea of hope slip in? What would they tell us about ourselves and what we can do to demonstrate our compassion to others?

There's a verse in the Old Testament that's one of my favorites. And not just for the reason you might think. Let me share the verse and then I'll tell ya why it's one of my favorites.

> But the Lord said to Samuel, "Do not consider his appearance or his height, for I have rejected him. The Lord does not look

at the things that people look at. People look at the outward appearance, but the Lord looks at the heart." (1 Samuel 16:7)

This is that part of the Bible where David was going to be anointed king. And David was "short in stature." I'm anywhere between five foot five and five foot seven, depending on the colored numbers on the door jambs of whichever convenience store I'm walking out of. So I can really identify with the idea of short people doing great things! But look what else is in this passage—we're told to look past the physical appearance and see the heart. When I think of what Shadow taught me, I'm humbled that a dog is that smart. She saw past my looks and saw my heart; she saw past my physical limitations and saw my heart. In fact, Shadow looked past everyone's looks and she saw their hearts. And that's why so many people saw her as a lover, a sweetheart of a dog. Bear demonstrated grace and dignity under the most difficult of times in his young life. People who came into our home initially saw a dog covered with sores and warts. They left in delight, knowing they met a dog with a heart that was bigger than they ever could have imagined. I'm told that feeling continued long after they left.

It'd be easy to say—to write—that life is tough and we need to get used to it, and in doing so we might find that sense of hope that we all long for. There are people who use sayings describing pulling up your bootstraps or "getting over it," whatever *it* is. I don't think it's that easy. I don't think all the despair we witness (and maybe experience) can be replaced so easily with hope. I think we need someone in our lives to show us hope, to help us find hope. When we hang onto hope, we find ways of climbing out of the hole that we all find ourselves in from time to time.

Looking at someone's heart—not their appearance.

Allowing others to look at our heart—not our appearance.

Can we do it?

Maybe in the days and weeks ahead, you and me, we can help others find hope. Heck, we can make a difference in the life of someone we might not even know. We've been shown how to do it, we've read about it—now we can be part of it. And if we're in need of hope, we know there's someone out there who sees past our defects, who sees beyond whatever physical appearance we might show. That person sees our heart. You might not realize it right away, but I have faith that every one of us has that someone in our lives.

More Good News, wouldn't you agree?

The Papilloma virus is clearly visible on Shadow's paws.

Bear, looking sad as he waits for some loving.

Eliot

…Where there is despair, hope…

When you need someone to lean on, it's reassuring to know there are people out there willing to make sacrifices in their own life to help make your life easier. That was the case when we needed someone to take Bear and Shadow when I went into the hospital. I can still remember that feeling of relief knowing we didn't have to beg other foster homes to take them, a group message went out to all the foster families and Mary saw that there was a need and she stepped up. It was nice knowing we wouldn't have to beg anyone to help us out, and that Taryn didn't have to ask another family to take Bear and Shadow.

Every foster family needs to take a break from time to time. You simply run the risk of burnout taking in dog after dog, or *dogs* after *dogs* if you're agreeing to take in more than one at a time. We were on one of those breaks, it was an extended break when Elissa took a call from Taryn. Another family was going on vacation and they had four foster dogs in their home at the time. In order for them to get a much-needed two-week holiday, those dogs had to be temporarily rehomed. We try not to put our foster dogs in a kennel except in the most extreme circumstances. If our organization can avoid boarding the dogs in our foster care, we will find a way, make a way, and even threaten to find a way. Elissa was asked if we could take two of the dogs.

I learned about this covert phone call later in the afternoon when Taryn called me to find out what time would work to drop the dogs off.

"I'm sorry, Taryn, drop *what* dogs off?"

"Elissa didn't tell you, did she?"

"Hold on, Taryn. I'll be right back."

Oh, Elissa, I think we need to talk…

It's hard to be mad at someone when they do something for the right reason, isn't it? How could I get angry at Elissa for opening her heart—and our front door—for a fellow foster family in need? It didn't take long to remember the sacrifice Mary made in her home by taking Bear and Shadow. So I just smiled. And wondered why Taryn called Elissa and not me.

You women really do stick together, don't you?

Well, our break was officially over when *Eliot* and his brother, *FedX*, were brought to our home by Rob and Jenn, the foster family heading out the next morning for Disney World. Eliot and FedX were the last two puppies born into our foster organization. Their momma arrived months earlier, pregnant and ready to deliver any day. Like almost all the other dogs who find their way into rescue organizations, their mom came from a high-kill shelter that was going to euthanize her, and her belly full of unborn puppies.

Four of their siblings had already been adopted, Eliot and Fedx were still waiting for someone to fall in love with, and give them their "fur-ever" home. They were twelve weeks old when they ran through our front door. Reportedly they were a Hound/Shepherd mix, with maybe a little bit of Labrador in them. To us they just looked adorable and we couldn't figure out why they hadn't been adopted yet. Elissa and I felt relieved that since they came from a loving foster family who took great care of them, they wouldn't need the usual baths that all the other foster dogs that came into our home got. We were off to a good start.

That lasted about an hour before I saw Eliot carrying around one of my slippers. It was one of a pair of slippers (funny how shoes are always sold like that) that Elissa had just bought for me. They were soft and comfortable. And not cheap. By the time I pried it out of his mouth, the shoe lace was eaten to shreds and the warm, fuzzy lining was chewed and soaked with slobber. No sooner did I put that away that Elissa found FedX gnawing at the center island in the kitchen. Bailey and the other dogs just looked on from a distance as if to say, "What did you expect was going to happen?"

Personally, I think our dogs could have stepped in and given us a hand. Maybe they could've barked? Something to get our attention? Nope, all they were concerned with was playing with the puppies in the backyard. And out they all went! We'd forgotten just how quickly things can turn from calm and serene to *all hell's breaking loose*. While the pack was outside burning off some of their energy, Elissa and I went around the house in an attempt to "puppy-proof" it as much as possible. After we were satisfied we'd done all we could do, we let them in and gave our dogs a chance to teach Eliot and FedX how things work at the Williams Canine Hotel.

Our dogs all sat in a line in front of the counter where the dog biscuits were kept. No one got anything until everyone was sitting calmly. At first Eliot and FedX didn't know what to make of this weird ritual. But as soon as they saw each dog getting a treat, they knew something good happens. It took a little while, as well as a lot of patience, but Elissa finally got both Eliot and FedX to sit—not at the same time (that would come later, much later), but they did sit. And when they sat, they received a nice little reward.

Phase 1 of establishing who's in control, as well as the concept of reward training, was now complete. On to Phase 2: What dog is in charge of maintaining foster dog decorum. That would be Bailey, and again, like with every other foster dog that came into our home, she did it without showing any aggression or dominance, and somehow each and every dog knew what her role was.

> Whoever said 'Let sleeping dogs
> lie' didn't sleep with dogs.
>
> —Unknown

Hey, this wasn't going that bad at all! Next up after playtime, bedtime. And I gotta tell ya, it was really nice having to share a bed with *only* three dogs for the time we were on hiatus from fostering. Eliot and FedX shared a large crate at their previous foster home and that crate was delivered with them. We were told they sleep in it together and there shouldn't be a problem. The crate was in the family room, our bedroom is on the second floor. We ushered them into the crate and said goodnight. Then we went upstairs to go to bed—Elissa, me, and the dogs. The cats were already there waiting for us.

After finding my sliver of the edge of the mattress, Elissa grabbed whatever blanket she could and tried to cover her shoulders on the other edge of the bed. The dogs had the middle to themselves. No sooner had the lights gone out that Elissa asked me, in a whispered voice, if I thought the puppies would be okay. I answered of course they were.

"But what if something happens? We won't hear it."

"Hun, they're fine. I promise they're going to be fine. Go to sleep."

"But don't you think it's unfair that our dogs are up here and Eliot and FedX have to stay downstairs?"

"Seriously?"

"I'm serious. I don't think it's fair at all."

"What do you want me to do?"

"Don't you think they should be up here with us?"

"What do you want me to do?"

"I'm asking you, don't you think they should be upstairs with all of us? Don't you think it's unfair?"

"If you think it's unfair then I think it's unfair. Let me go get their crate and bring it up here."

"But you...you don't think they should sleep with us?"

"Where?"

"In bed. In bed with everyone else."

"Sure. Why not..."

Three dogs, two cats, and two new puppies later, and we were all set for a good night's sleep. We were *set* for a good night's sleep, that didn't mean it actually happened. That's because our newest fosters thought being on the bed was really cool and they wanted to play. They wanted to play with the dogs. They wanted to play with the cats. They wanted to play with Elissa. They wanted to play with me.

Exhausted after that first night doesn't come close to describing how my body felt. Now five bowls needed to be filled instead of three, and it was only seven o'clock in the morning. Oh, how much I'd forgotten…

Within two weeks, an application had come in for FedX. We'd blasted their pictures all over Facebook and one of Corey's friends saw them. He wanted to come over and see FedX, so he completed the online application and once that was approved, he came over. Rob stayed more than two hours playing with FedX and Eliot, learning everything he could about them. Although Elissa and I tried to convince him to take both puppies, the rules of his apartment complex permitted only one dog. And he really hit it off with FedX. Two days later, Corey and I were driving to Rob's house with FedX in the back seat.

Eliot was now the last puppy in the litter who still hadn't been adopted. I don't know if he was the runt of the litter, but he certainly wasn't the alpha dog. When he and FedX played, he was always the one being dominated. Their play got rougher as the weeks went on. It got so rough that there were times Eliot cried out in pain, FedX was biting him that hard. When they arrived in our house, we noticed Eliot had scabs on his neck and back. As we watched the way they played, it became obvious that FedX played to win and he'd bite Eliot on the back and hold him down by his neck. This went on all day, every day. For as long as FedX (who was a sweet dog with a great disposition) was in our home, he took charge of Eliot. We wondered again if Eliot was the runt of the litter.

> Rambunctious, rumbustious, delinquent dogs become
> angelic when sitting.
>
> —Dr. Ian Dunbar

With FedX gone, Eliot was able to be himself. He no longer had to worry about his brother jumping on him, ambushing him around every corner. Eliot could just be Eliot and play with the other dogs who weren't there to dominate him or cause any problems. Yep, no problems for Eliot to deal with. You know why? Because Eliot found enough problems on his own:

- Another pair of slippers—well, just one of them but it was the same foot as the first pair, so I was still screwed.
- Baseboard moldings.
- Staircase treads (the nosing—that curved part hanging over each riser).
- Cord to my electric shaver.
- Cord to the vacuum cleaner.
- Cord to a videogame system.
- Videogame controller.
- One of Elissa's paintings.
- Elissa's sneakers.
- Two cell phone chargers.
- Corey's wallet.
- Railing on the deck.
- Screwdriver.
- Computer power cord (to *this* laptop!)
- A bunch of things I forgot...

Eliot was, how you say, *curious*. He was cute, adorable, loveable... and curious. He was curious about *everything*! And it was that curiosity that made him so much fun to be around. Did you ever watch a puppy go outside? Everything is new to them. It's like when Eliot went outside he was experiencing it all for the first time. Every time. Just watching him follow a leaf falling to the ground—he was in awe of it. He chased it and tried to grab it out of the air. And when he missed on the first try, he didn't give up, he went right back after it. Wind be damned, he was determined to get this thing that fell from the sky.

I've been accused of waking up in the same mood every day. I wake up and I'm happy. I don't see the big deal, if I wake up and my feet hit the floor, that day is Thanksgiving. When you wake up with "an attitude of gratitude," the day seems to go your way. Are there days that I don't feel that great? Sure! But just because a part of the day, the beginning, isn't great, that doesn't mean I can't look forward to the possibilities of what the rest of the day will bring. Does it sound crazy? Maybe, but I think we all have a responsibility to others around us, especially our friends and loved ones. We can't promise to feel a certain way, but we can promise to act a certain way.

Waking up to Eliot licking my face is something I miss to this day. He'd wake up and his tail was wagging. Just like that, he was awake and he was happy about it. Elissa and I were happier than him if we could get him outside before he had an accident on the floor!

Eliot would run around with the other dogs and you could see how excited they all were to be outside. They looked forward to just being outside. Eliot didn't stop his good-natured fun when he came back inside. In fact, that fun (and curiosity) continued all day long. It's amazing, dogs wake up in the same mood every day, a great mood. They expect that the day is going to be a good one; they have no thoughts of anything but what this particular day has to offer. Seems we can learn a lot from dogs.

If we can learn from dogs, can dogs learn from us? God, I hope so. If you've ever watched a dog, you soon realize that they learn a lot from their environment, and if that environment has cats in it, you can bet that a dog will learn from them. Eliot was no exception.

When he and FedX first saw Bellagio and Bojangles, they had no idea what to make of these strange creatures. It didn't take long for our two cats to demonstrate why felines rule the wild animal kingdom. Before I go any further, you need to know that both cats have no front claws, they're both inside cats. And no puppies were harmed in the making of the next paragraph.

As stated in an earlier chapter, Bellagio and Bojangles became experts in determining just how close they could get to any new dog in our house and they knew every escape route by heart. Almost every one of those escape routes included using height to their advantage. They would simply jump on something higher than the dogs could reach. This might be a piece of furniture, a counter, and on some extreme situations, the top of our kitchen cabinets. But when the situation was more a nuisance in their mind, they would stand on a counter or piece of furniture and then beat the living snot out of the dog's face with their paws. It looked like a lopsided boxing match, the kind where the opponent doesn't know whether to bob or weave.

And again, since they were declawed, there was never any injury to any of the dogs, it was just entertainment for us to watch. FedX and Eliot soon learned that by chasing the cats, they had playmates for as long as they wanted their snouts smacked because the cats never got tired of letting them know who was in charge. The advantage became even more obvious after FedX was adopted. Now, not only was it a feline power play, but it was two against one—Bellagio and Bojangles against Eliot. I have to hand it to the little guy, Eliot wasn't one to give up when faced with insurmountable odds. He pressed on, but he kept leading with his nose instead of how I tried to teach him. A polished fighter *never* leads with his nose...

The cats, especially Bojangles, taught Eliot one more thing that proved challenging for him: they taught him how to leap from object to object. Whether from dresser to dresser, counter to counter, or sofa to newel post, Eliot witnessed just how far cats can leap. He got to see their amazing vertical leap as well.

This was all new to Eliot, who, until he lived in our home, never saw a cat in his young life. And I would imagine it looked like fun—leaping across the kitchen floor instead of walking on it, jumping to and from different pieces of bedroom furniture, and somehow sticking the landing on that post at the top of the stairs. I can only guess at how many things were going through his head, but one thing that I am sure of is he saw this as a challenge. And Eliot was rapidly showing us he was not one to back down from a challenge.

Our first glimpse of his determination to be like a cat was watching TV one evening. Elissa and I were relaxing on the chairs and the dogs were resting on whatever piece of furniture was available to them. Eliot was on the love seat when he must have seen an antler on the ottoman that Bailey left behind. Without any warning, Eliot leaped from the love seat and landed on the ottoman, about four feet away from the sofa. We couldn't believe what we just saw! But this would be just the start of things to come.

The more Eliot chased Bojangles on the counter in the kitchen, the more Bojangles jumped over his head going from one part of the kitchen to the other. Eliot stood there watching a cat seemingly flying in the air right over his head. Eliot jumped up and tried to do the same. Didn't work nearly as good as the cat.

So we now were watching a cat flying through the air in the kitchen, launching over a puppy who was on his hind legs trying to get airborne. And then said puppy would do his own thing in the living room and family room—launching from one couch to another, running full speed onto a sofa and with that momentum, he'd jump across the room onto another piece of furniture. He never seemed to tire of this, but the other dogs did. And Bailey, being the canine enforcer in the home, would run up to him and bark. We assume this was in an attempt to get him to stop. Her barks fell on deaf ears as Eliot continued this indoor gym play until Elissa or I stopped him. It wasn't that we didn't enjoy watching it, we were afraid he would hurt himself if he missed one of his intended targets.

And still, after all this time,
the Sun has never said to the Earth, "You owe me."
Look what happens with love like that.
It lights up the sky.

—Hafiz

What was supposed to be a few short weeks turned into months and months of trying to get Eliot adopted. There was a lot of interest, but no one pulled the trigger and completed an adoption application on him. This created more than one problem, the first being we were really starting to fall for this guy. He grew in our hearts as he continued to grow in size. And unless you want a house full of your own personal dogs, this can be a dangerous thing. The other problem was that he was getting accustomed to our way of doing things. This could make it harder for him to get used to doing things the way his new (future) family operated. That can lead to confusion and behavioral problems if one is not careful. So our concern was not without merit.

When a dog becomes part of your family, as all our foster dogs did, certain changes take place in your heart. One is of acceptance. Another change that happens is a slow melting of your heart. These changes are amplified when you're not feeling well. I don't know what you think of coincidences, but I tend to see them in what has become a fairly well known quote attributed to Albert Einstein: "Coincidence is God's way of remaining anonymous." I'm not asking you to agree with this statement, or agree with anything for that matter. I believe having an open mind is more important than thinking we're right. But just for a moment, think about how it must feel when you're feeling lousy and a dog arrives that seems to be able to sense your aches and pains. That's what happened with Eliot and me. It was because of a whole lot of aches and pains in this old body that Elissa and I took a break from fostering. When Eliot arrived in our home, the last thing I thought I needed was another dog to take care of. Or another thing that Elissa needed to take care of in addition to her other responsibilities, *and stress*, of dealing with everything she had going on with me.

Look, either this was an amazing coincidence or something was going on that I didn't know about. Either way, Eliot helped me in ways he could never have imagined. Nor could any of us who had been a part of his young life up until this point. I'm in pain, not just some of the time, I'm in pain *all* of the time. The only variable is the number (as doctors like to scale it) of my pain level. Medications and operations to implant devices in me help, but nothing completely takes away the pain I'm in.

And while Eliot didn't take away my pain, he did give me a break from it. Eliot was the distraction I needed at the very time I needed it the most. For the past four and half years my back pain has been getting gradually worse, the increase in pain (and conversely, the decline in my quality of life) couldn't be measured in days or weeks, or even months. It had to be measured year by year. If I were to look back at each passing week, I wouldn't be able to evaluate how much the pain increased. I could only say that I was in less pain this time last year. And that type of evaluation would continue for me for the next four years.

The summer Eliot arrived in our home was different. The pain was getting worse on a regular basis. My quality of life was decreasing in a measurable way that I hadn't been able to see before that summer. That's why I thought the last thing we needed was a new puppy in the house. I soon learned how wrong I was.

We were on high alert from the minute he and his brother arrived. There wasn't a moment we couldn't take our minds off what he and his brother were doing. We were constantly thinking of what we had to do next, of what we had to "Eliot-proof" next. And when I say *constantly*, I mean constantly. When we failed to keep our minds going, Eliot certainly had a way of reminding us. A simple review of the bulleted list a few pages back should give you an idea of how he reminded us!

So when he wasn't sleeping, we were busy. It was almost like having a baby where your sleep schedule revolved around theirs. You slept when they slept. Chasing a puppy around all day, every day, will certainly give you something to think about other than your own problems. That's for sure. But Eliot did more than cause enough problems that neither one of us (or our kids) got any rest, he discovered a way to help me feel better by snuggling next to me when I felt like crap. Eliot seemed to have a built-in barometer of sorts that sensed when my pain level was up; when I was in pain, he was next to me. Not on the floor next to me, he was *next to me*. Like sharing the chair next to me.

There's a reason most hospitals have programs that allow therapy dogs into patient's rooms. Dogs have a way of not only breaking down barriers, but building up people in the process. They have an uncanny ability of turning a dark day into something meaningful. And when we think of something positive, it's difficult to feel something negative. Go ahead, give it a try: think of a memory that makes you happy. Now remember that and try to feel down. Sure, you might be able to feel down immediately after that thought from your past, but in that moment, you couldn't feel down. It's just the way our brains are wired. By the way, the reverse is also true: try to think of something that's sad, something that brought misery to your life. I bet you didn't (couldn't) smile when you were thinking of that. We really do become what we think. I think, at least I'm pretty sure.

If you know someone who's in chronic pain, you know what their day consists of. It revolves around pain. Whether it's a lot of pain where you can't do anything, a little bit of pain where you're able to get things done, or hoping you don't have excruciating pain later when you want to do something. Everything revolves around pain. So it's more than just a distraction when your day is able to revolve around something other than pain. Something that gives your life a sense of worth—to be needed—is much more than a distraction. It's a lifesaver!

With Eliot next to me, I felt needed, probably because he needed someone to pet him and he let me know it. So instead of feeling sorry for myself, I felt useful. I was needed. At least my fingers were needed. And when the momentum of Eliot's weight caused the furniture to move when he leapt from one piece to another, I was needed to nudge them back to their original spots. I figured Eliot had the jumps measured to the inch and I didn't want to see him miss, so I would walk around the rooms he just left, nudging sofas and ottomans back to where they were before Eliot started his routine.

And of course, Eliot needed someone to feed him and give him his treats, and Elissa was kind enough to allow me to assist her in this task. There really is a deep bond created when you feed another creature, isn't there? When someone or something is dependent on you, the relationship is either strengthened or weakened. It becomes weakened when score is kept, when we think who owes who on a quid-pro-quo basis. It never balances out, does it? But when we stop keeping score and understand our dependence on one another, magical things happen.

Eliot never felt (as far as I know) like he was mooching a free meal off of me. He understood that I—and every one of us—was there to take care of him, to give him shelter and food. And I didn't feed him hoping to get something in return, I didn't hold him accountable for anything in return for me feeding him. I needed to understand what my role was as well. And in life, those roles can change at a moment's notice, and often do. One minute we're the one who is doing the feeding (taking care of another) and the next thing we know we find ourselves in a situation where we're the ones needing to be fed. We're the ones dependent on another.

Going into that summer, I never would have guessed things would go downhill so quick. I never thought there would be days as dark as the ones that led up to Eliot coming into our lives. And I never could have guessed that a puppy, filled with more energy than all the dogs in our house at that time, would bring me out of that darkness. It's unimaginable that a dog can make you forget about what's bothering you, or how much pain you're in. Or is it?

In his book, *Being Mortal*, Dr. Atul Gawande notes different studies that demonstrates how patients thrive when they have something to take care of, be it a plant, a bird, a cat, or a dog. He recounts an interview with a director of a nursing home who allowed all these into his facility and then, two years after this groundbreaking idea, the effects were studied. Researchers compared quality of life with another nursing home in the area and the results were astounding: prescription requirements were half of that of the control nursing home; psychotropic drugs for agitation were down considerably; total drug costs were just 38 percent of the comparison facility, and deaths fell by 15 percent.

In short, when people have a purpose to live, they live not just longer, but better. In some cases, *much* better. So obvious it makes you go, "Duh!" And yet, we find ourselves amazed again and again at how much pets contribute to our lives, as if we're surprised. At least that was the case with me. Having grown up with pets all my life, and having worked with dogs for more than three decades, I should have known this. I wondered if I had begun to take so much for granted.

When we get in that dark place, it can be hard to see any light. And if we do see light, often we're seduced into not trusting it. We look for reasons to doubt it instead of reaching for it. And then, seemingly out of nowhere, something (occasionally with four legs) gets dropped right into our laps. If we're lucky, that thing cuddles in our laps once it arrives.

It makes you wonder, doesn't it? If something as innocent as a helpless puppy can bring light into our lives, what else is possible? What else, or who else, can bring light into our lives? Where could we look to find it? When you think about it, the possibilities are endless!

Eliot taught me that there are always reasons to, quoting Monty Python, "Look on the bright side of life." His love for life was infectious, his curiosity contagious, and yet his looks were benign. There was nothing about his looks that made you think he was the best looking or the ugliest dog. Just an average looking pup with a huge heart, the kind of mutt that melts your heart.

When I think of the times my heart's been melted, I can't help but remember it was because something, or someone, gave me a reason to think about them and not me. Maybe when we think of someone other than ourselves, we open our hearts to seeing a light that shines where before we saw nothing. I doubt I'm the only one who's seen something special in someone, but when I mentioned it to them, they shunned the idea and replied that they didn't see anything special in themselves. And what about us, you and me?

Have you ever had someone tell you they saw something special in you but you rejected it outright?

Perhaps you and me, we can continue this journey by understanding that when we shine a light on others, we light up their lives in ways we could never imagine; we literally put light where darkness once lived in their hearts. And when we have an opportunity to help another living creature that is dependent on us, may we always think of puppies like Eliot who unknowingly shine a light were darkness once lived. It's a reminder of the Good News that bounds from sofa to chair to kitchen counter, joy that shines a light in your life and in mine.

Eliot enjoys people furniture as much
(or more than) his human foster parents.

Rosie

"Once upon a time there was a princess who…"
"Once upon a time in a faraway land, there was a tiny kingdom…"
"Once upon a time there lived a…"
"And they lived happily ever after!"

According to the Oxford English Dictionary, the stock phrase *once upon a time* has been used at least 1,380 times in (English language) storytelling. We all know how these stories end; more often than not the fairy tales we've heard since childhood end with, "And they lived happily ever after."

That happens only in fairy tales, right? I mean, in real life, the ugly duckling doesn't see herself as a beautiful swan in the end. Most of the time the ugly ducklings in our life remain ugly ducklings; be they the homeless, the lost, the addict, the unwed mother, the bastard child, the immigrant, the depressed, or the physically deformed. As I'm writing this there's a national headline of a ninety-year-old man and two ministers being arrested in Fort Lauderdale, Florida, for violating a city ordinance by feeding the homeless. We tend to find ways to push the "ugly" out of our sight at almost any cost.

This is a straightforward story of a dog named Rosie. This is a true story. It's not a childhood fairy tale written by Hans Christian Andersen, this is her story. And it's our story.

Let's work this backward then forward, from the finish to the beginning and then back to see how it ends. Here's a blog, written by Rosie's human adopter the night she brought Rosie home from our house:

Pretty Is, As Pretty Does!

Beauty is not in the face; beauty is a light in the heart—so said Kahlil Gibran. See…all my life I've sought the beautiful—in music, in art, in photography, in objects to paint. Which doesn't mean that everyone else has to agree with me—but at least I found these things aesthetically lovely.

To my mind there is no more beautiful dog than a golden retriever. The sight of a golden standing in the wind with fur and feathers blowing just grabs my heart. I have been fortunate in having two beautiful Golden Retrievers. My first, Hannah, lived to 12, and my current Golden, Miriam Rose, is 13 1/4. I had promised myself when Miriam died, I would adopt a shelter dog, but I had some strong preferences. I wanted a large dog with soft fluffy fur, with some of the Golden loveliness in her. But I imagine the Divine mind had something else planned—a life lesson to be learned.

I brought home last night a shelter dog who had been in a wonderful foster home. She came from a [high] kill-shelter, and was the only one not going to be transported north for adoption. She heralded her arrival to my house by nervously leaving a trail of pee through three rooms! Rosie is her current name, and no one was rushing to adopt her because she is 2 yrs. old, and because she will never win a beauty contest. She has a corgi body—white with brown blotches, freckled bowed legs, an optical problem called *cherry eye* in one eye, and her lower jaw is thrust out so her lower teeth jut out as well. She couldn't be any more opposite from what I envisioned! But she is a gentle, loving little girl—and after a while, you begin to see her as beautiful. A wonderful example of the old adage, "You can't judge a book by its cover."

This isn't the first time I've been treated to God's particular brand of humor! Fortunately, I can laugh right along! Things aren't definite yet since we're trying this out to see if the two dogs can get along. But I suspect that the dapper Rosie has found a new home.

And they lived happily ever after…

Right? I can report that Rosie did indeed stay at that home, she was adopted by a wonderful woman who is dear to our hearts.

Every great ending has to have a beginning. Now that we know how it ends, let's go back to the beginning. This is the story of how it all started, of how *they lived happily ever after.*

Elissa and I were notified of an upcoming transport where our rescue organization would be pulling dogs from more than one shelter in a southern state where the euthanasia rate was among the highest in the country. Time was of the essence and the shelters weren't just taking a verbal commitment to spare the dog's lives; they were going to euthanize these animals on a certain date at a certain time regardless of any promises by rescue groups to pull them.

What happens most of the time is that rescue organizations get "urgent euth lists." These are lists from shelters across the country that publish the names and brief descriptions of dogs who are scheduled to be euthanized. These descriptions include the breed (if not known, what the dog is believed or appears to be), age, temperament, health, any behavior issues, and if there is a history of human aggression or bites. A picture is included in each description.

Taryn called me at home while Elissa was at work and told me that all of the dogs that we (our organization) were pulling had foster homes ready for them. There was just one issue that Taryn wanted to run by me: One of the shelters we were pulling from advised her that all but one of the dogs on their euth list were being sent to various rescue groups. Just one dog was going to be put down, all the other dogs had rescue organizations coming for them. When Taryn heard this she called me...

What was I supposed to say? Especially after she emailed me a picture of *the one dog* that was going to be put to sleep in a few days. The only issues we could think of why this one dog didn't get pulled by any other rescue were her age and her looks. And those are two biggies. There was no mention of any behavior issues. In fact, this dog was said to be very friendly. Nothing about dog or human aggression and no major health issues. The only health issue was what is called a *cherry eye*. A cherry eye is a bulging of a tear duct in the corner of the eye, it looks painful (and weird), but isn't considered life-threatening and is painless in most dogs. The other issue was her age—older dogs have a harder time being adopted and this dog was more than two years old.

> Love does not consist of gazing at each other,
> but looking outward together in the same direction.
>
> —Antoine de Saint-Exupery

I'll ask you again, knowing all that I just shared, in addition to a picture of this dog tugging at my heart, what was I supposed to say? I said yes and sent Elissa an email to her work, explaining the situation and asking for her to understand why I said yes. I followed that up with a second email with the picture of Rosie attached. Almost immediately I received a reply from Elissa. She thought Rosie looked adorable and didn't care about her age (which could mean an extended foster period). I was told I made the right decision. Yes, a wife told her husband he made the right decision; I was tempted to note the date and time—just in case I needed it for future evidence.

Nah, I was never worried. We were a team, still are. And as long as a decision is made out of love, we support that decision. Phew, thank God!

Of all the dogs we fostered up to that point, this one felt *the most right*, if that's a correct use of the English vernacular. It was always good to know that we were saving dogs, and that we were part of an organization committed to doing the same. But we never had an opportunity to take the one dog out of an entire shelter that was going to be killed if *we* didn't take it. That was a lot to digest. I have to admit, it was almost too overwhelming to think about. An entire shelter was going to be cleared out of all the dogs who were scheduled to be put down, except for one dog. I can't imagine what it must have felt like for Rosie if she knew what was going on. Could you put yourself in her position? What would that feel like if you knew you were the only dog not wanted? And on top of that, because you weren't wanted, you were going to be put to sleep. Makes ya think, doesn't it?

Rosie arrived well after dinnertime, since the transport vehicles were changed twice on the way up to New Jersey. The first caravan brought them part of the way, then the next caravan picked them up and took them to a staging point north of us where both our organization and other rescues took their preassigned dogs and brought them to their respective locations. By the time Rosie and the other dogs coming into our rescue arrived, it was past seven o'clock. We were sure she hadn't eaten, so Elissa cooked up her special "welcome to our home" canine meal for her. Rosie ignored the other dogs as she enjoyed her first meal in presumably a full day.

As hard as it is to admit, I was a little grossed out when I first saw Rosie. It was that thing on her eye, it looked like it was so uncomfortable and all I could think of is how that would feel if it was in *my* eye. In my four years as a paramedic and twenty-five as a police officer, I witnessed my fair share of trauma. Trauma calls were the most challenging for me and I enjoyed that challenge as both a paramedic and a cop. But the one type of trauma that I never got used to, the one kind of call that made my knees weak, was eye injuries. I could see a lot of sick stuff, but something in the eye, and I was almost worthless to my partner. I think it came from an incident during my childhood when my brother aimed an air rifle at me and pulled the trigger. Before he pointed it at me, he shoved it in the ground and a plug of dirt was lodged in the end of the barrel. When he pulled the trigger, the glob of moist dirt struck me right in the eye. I didn't know what pain was until that moment in my young life. And ever since then, nothing could go near my eyes and anything in anyone else's eye grossed me out—including contact lenses. I don't know how you guys do it!

Once I got past her eye, what I noticed was a dog that wasn't shy, but also wasn't aggressive at all. She was assertive with the other dogs, but showed no aggression toward them. Rosie walked around our home like she owned it, she didn't strut, but her gait reflected confidence. She was also overweight. We assumed, based on her disposition and body mass, that she might have belonged to a senior citizen who overfed her. Perhaps her former owner moved into a facility that didn't allow dogs, maybe her owner got sick and could no longer care for her, or maybe her owner had died. The sending shelter had no information on Rosie, so these were all guesses.

For her size and shape—short legs and barrel-chested—Rosie ran and jumped with no problem. You might expect a dog with short, stubby legs to not be able to keep up with dogs who had longer legs and weren't overweight. But Rosie ran in the yard and chased them just like any other dog we had. And when it came time to sleep, Rosie had no trouble making the jump up onto our bed.

Where Rosie really excelled, however, was her molding to your body position wherever you sat. If you were in a chair, Rosie would climb up and sit on your lap. Then she would cuddle up to you and take the shape of your body. Her body matched the contours of your body, like putty or clay. In fact, I seriously thought of renaming her *Clay* because she literally molded to everyone's body. If you were lying on the couch, same thing—just in a more horizontal position. Her reputation grew both in our house and out; friends and family who visited wanted to sit with Rosie and feel her love.

All you had to do was start rubbing her belly, and you could be assured that she wasn't moving for anything. And she was like this with everyone. Elissa tried her best to get Rosie to see her as her favorite. It didn't happen. I tried the same thing, same results. Both Matt and Corey made valiant efforts as well, but all that did was give them aching arms as they ended up petting her for hours with nothing to show for it. It was almost like Rosie was intent on proving to everyone that she wasn't going to be exclusively loyal to anyone. She had no favorites in our house in the weeks and months that followed, she simply enjoyed the touch of a human next to her. And all she asked in return for sharing her love was a gentle stroke of your fingers on her belly.

Rosie's refusal to show favoritism to anyone began to change with the regular visits of the associate pastor from our church. Ginny started coming over to get help from Matt and Elissa on her new blog. She was starting a blog and needed some guidance getting it up and running. And since she was born in the same era as Elissa and I where we didn't grow up with technology, Matt seemed like the perfect person to help her out. Elissa taught web design and graphic design, so her expertise was invaluable as well. I just stood back and made believe I understood what they were talking about.

Ginny visited with us every Thursday evening after dinner. Everyone in the house began looking forward to our "Thursday's with Ginny" as we affectionately called them (referring to the title from Mitch Album's bestselling book, *Tuesday's With Morrie*). Not only did us humans look forward to the visits, but the four-legged family members couldn't wait as well. And it didn't take long for the dogs to start getting antsy by the front door around seven o'clock every Thursday night. How they knew, we didn't know. Maybe it was Elissa getting the water going so Ginny could have her cup of tea when she arrived. Who knows? All we knew is every member of our family—two- and four-legged ones—looked forward to these visits.

Once the blog was up and running, the visits turned to more personal topics where we began to share each other's lives with one another. We shared in confidence, not ever worrying that we might be embarrassed later on. And we shared just about everything—our successes, our failures, our fears, and especially our faith. Ginny gave Elissa and me the strength to question things and move forward in our faith journey. Together we examined scripture and ancient history, we talked about what might be possible and where we might end up. It was both challenging and enlightening as we stretched our minds. We forced them to open up to things we never would have considered if not for Ginny's encouragement and support. Not only did we share desserts, tea, and an occasional dinner, we shared trust in each other's lives.

Of the four dogs now in our home, Rosie was the one who, from the beginning, showed the most interest in Ginny. And guess what? Ginny began showing preference to Rosie. We'd sit in the family room or living room, and once seated, Rosie made sure she was the first dog standing in front of Ginny. It wasn't long before Ginny invited Rosie up on the sofa with her and the rest of the night was spent talking and laughing, all with Rosie curled up against Ginny. Just like modeling clay.

One Thursday night Elissa joked with Ginny that since Rosie loved her, Ginny should take her home. Ginny replied that she already had a dog at home, and she was an older dog. Besides, she didn't want the responsibilities of another dog just yet. A week later, after witnessing more of the same love between them, Elissa said that Rosie *looked* like she belonged to Ginny. And since Rosie picked Ginny over anyone else to sit with, she might as well bite the bullet and get it over with—just adopt her, for Pete's sake! Nope, not ready yet, was Ginny's response.

As the weeks went on, Ginny's defenses were taking a beating by Rosie's persistence. Now it wasn't enough for Rosie to just sit with Ginny, Rosie began kissing her while cuddling with her. Uh-oh…

Although Ginny never mentioned it, we saw a subtle change in the way she talked to Rosie. And we found our conversations turning to dog issues and stories. This, mixed with a healthy dose of theology, makes for some interesting banter. I think Ginny knew a few weeks before she finally asked that she'd fallen for Rosie and had to find a way to make her a part of her family.

Now might be a good time to go back a few pages and reread Ginny's blog, the one she wrote the night she took Rosie home. Go ahead, I'll wait…

Did Ginny see something in Rosie? Was she able to see past her eye, past her physical appearance, and see Rosie's heart? Did the ugly duckling realize she was a swan all along?

I think the answers to these questions are, in the order they were asked: Yes. Yes. And yes.

Something magical happens when we allow love in, doesn't it? We didn't know why Rosie didn't show favoritism to anyone in our home, and it wasn't as if she was aloof or disinterested. Just the opposite was true of Rosie—she was one of the most loving and affectionate dogs we ever fostered. She loved *everyone*! And she loved the dogs as well, nothing got her riled. She totally ignored the cats and played with the dogs when she wanted—on her terms. She acted like the mature one in the pack, like a group of ornery teenagers where one member of that group was thinking smarter than the rest and who was obviously the more mature one, the one who made the right decisions. It's not like this one member didn't want to associate with the others, she did. She enjoyed their company and she was a loyal friend. This one member just had her act together and everyone the group came across immediately recognized this girl as the one who established herself as not having to go along with everyone else just because they were her friends. You know that type of person, teenager, don't you?

We had to wonder if Rosie was simply waiting for the right person to come along. Ginny was getting ready to retire from the ministry. After more than four decades of helping so many people, Ginny was nearing that decision to retire. You should know she helped countless young people as a school teacher before entering the ministry. She devoted her life to helping others and now she might be lonely in the years after retirement. If not for Rosie, she might have been very lonely—her Miriam Rose died shortly after she adopted Rosie.

Part of Ginny's hesitating to adopt Rosie was her concern for Miriam Rose, as she didn't know if Miriam would accept her. Some years before, Ginny tried to bring another dog into the house, but her Miriam rejected that dog and there were some aggression issues. Ginny would later tell us this wasn't the case with Rosie. Miriam accepted her into the home and they got along great. Could Miriam have known that she was sick and that Ginny would need someone to fill that void after she was gone? Did Miriam sense something in Rosie that told her, "She's the one?" I would imagine there are skeptics who would argue this was all just one big coincidence— Rosie not attaching herself to anyone in particular until Ginny came into her life; Ginny wanting to adopt a rescue dog that was a large breed with a soft, wavy coat; Miriam becoming sicker as Ginny and

Rosie got to know each other better; Ginny making the decision when she did to take Rosie home for a trial run; Miriam accepting Rosie into their home; Miriam dying shortly before Ginny decided to retire. All of those things came together in just the right order for Rosie to be where she is today. And it all started with Ginny needing help with an online blog. I believe it was Einstein who said there are two ways to live your life: One is as though nothing is a miracle. The other is as though everything is a miracle.

> Dogs come into our lives to teach us about love, they depart
> to teach us about love.
> A new dog never replaces an old dog;
> it merely expands the heart.
> If you have loved many dogs, your heart is very big.
>
> —E. Jong

What starts out as dark often leads to periods of insight. Sometimes that's how we grow. What could have been the darkest day in Rosie's life turned into the light of ours—the day she arrived in our home. What could have been some of the darkest days in Ginny's life turned into a time of enlightenment. The darkness we all feel inside us from one time or another tends to mask opportunities for growth and understanding; we look at something that makes us feel uncomfortable and that darkness seeps into our decision making. We consciously decide to turn away from that which makes us uneasy in order to make ourselves feel more at ease. It's a nice feeling, it doesn't take much effort. But the feeling can seem empty.

When I first saw the picture of Rosie that Taryn sent me, I said to myself that her eye didn't look that bad. And then when I saw it in person...I was shocked. I wanted to turn away, I wanted to *not* deal with it—or her. It wasn't until I opened myself up to the possibility that she was more than a strange-looking eye (and lower jaw) that I saw her for who she really was. I allowed those dark feelings of uneasiness to basically blind me from the light of her love. Maybe that was what made Rosie special, maybe her love (not the mushy, slobbering kind that Eiko showed) lit something inside of everyone who met her, and in doing so, those people were able to shove that same darkness away that I felt and opened themselves to what was possible when they saw Rosie in her true light.

I'm not sure that's what happened with Ginny, though. I don't think she ever felt uneasy around Rosie, I think that's just the way Ginny is. She finds the beauty in what life has to offer, regardless of the outward appearance. And with Rosie, she demonstrated that for me in a way that was both eye-opening and humbling.

When you're a minister, you're supposed to lead by example. But my past experience as a kid with an air rifle clouded my vision, both literally and figuratively. It's been said that we're all the sum of our past experiences. Maybe we don't have to be a slave to them, however. Maybe we can learn from them and allow them to serve a purpose for learning more about ourselves and the world around us.

Rosie and Ginny's love for Rosie serve a purpose for learning about the importance of letting light in. Of flipping the switch that helps us see clearer. I can't imagine what it must have been like for Rosie when she was dropped off at that shelter months earlier. We probably all have a picture in our own minds of what that could've looked like. While we each have our own unique vision of that place, we all probably share a similar feeling about it—it was dark. The atmosphere was dark, the mood was dark, the feelings were dark, and Rosie was facing darkness with each passing day that she wasn't claimed from her concrete and metal wire room.

You and I share in the Good News that is Rosie's life. We share in the joy in Ginny's wisdom of seeing Rosie for who she was and who she was meant to be. It wasn't that long after she adopted Rosie that her Miriam Rose died. So it's safe to assume that Rosie arrived in her new home just at the right time. And that's the kind of story where they really do *live happily ever after.*

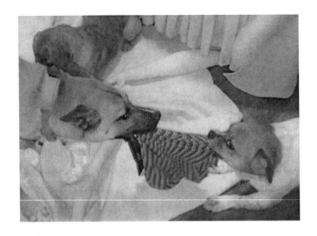

Eiko and Rosie find an unusual item to use to play tug-of-war: a pair of the author's underpants!

How can anyone not love Rosie's looks?

Bailey

I signed up for Aikido lessons after completing a defensive tactics course while I was a police officer. Aikido seemed to be the right martial art to study as a police officer because I figured I wouldn't need to know how to break a board or do a spinning roundhouse kick if I ever found myself in a bar fight. Most police officers are injured making arrests or subduing unruly people, and the fights they find themselves in are hand-to-hand, close-quarter battles where *fighting for your life* takes on a very real meaning. A police officer fighting to retain control of his own gun is something that can't be taken lightly.

Learning wrist locks, pressure points, and throws would serve me better than other styles of self-defense that were available in my area. I walked into the dojo for the first time and witnessed men and women dressed in funny robes with different colored belts tied around their waists. The instructor—the sensei—positioned all the newer students at the front of the room, while the more experienced students filled in the ranks behind us. I later learned that this is how things work in the *dojo* (literally translated from Japanese as "Place of the Way"). Newer students are seated (everyone sits *seiza*) during the opening of class and the place of honor was reserved for new students and students who weren't yet advanced in rank. Those students of higher rank sat in order of their ranks, working their way backward until the black belt students were in the last row. This idea of new(er) students sitting up front came from traditional Japanese customs where guests sit up front or at the best place at the table. The thought behind this was to make the guest feel welcome and to demonstrate that family members, those comfortable in the home, sacrifice their place for another. Even if that person was a complete stranger.

The sensei, or teacher, was a master at the art we were there to learn. He was treated with respect and honor, but he didn't act like he was better than anyone. In fact, he professed to each of us at every lesson that he was also a student, and always would be a student. The founder of Aikido, Morihei Ueshiba, considered himself to be a student until he died. In fact, he said that one never fully masters the art of Aikido; one of his sayings was, "Always a student." It reminded everyone, teachers especially, to remain humble in practicing the martial art he developed.

As I moved up in rank, I learned skills that would serve me well until I retired. And as I learned new skills, I developed a sense of pride in the culture and traditions of this martial art that was unknown in this country until the early 1950s. When I was asked to be an instructor of law enforcement officers who would learn special wrist locks, blocks, and throws, as well as handcuffing techniques, my sensei advised me to be careful. He reminded me that I was still a student and would always be a student. That helped me remain humble when the students—from various federal, state, and local law enforcement agencies—referred to me as a master of what we were working on. My sensei's advice, and that of Morihei Ueshiba, rang in my ears and reminded me of the importance of staying humble. No matter how much we think we know, there is always someone who knows more.

> My dog is usually pleased with what I do,
> because she is not infected with the
> concept of what I "should" be doing.
>
> —Lonzo Idolswine

We tend to look up to masters, don't we? We give credence to those who've mastered their craft, we respect those who are "masterful" at what they do. Oftentimes we set personal goals to master something, be it information for a test, a hobby or skill, maybe even a relationship issue. I know I'd like to devote more effort into mastering the art of forgiveness. If you could master one thing in your life, what would it be? Or, put another way: If you knew you wouldn't fail, what's the one thing in life you would like to try?

That last question reminded me of a very important and wise saying: "If at first you don't succeed, *do not* take up skydiving!"

Elissa and I didn't know if our genius idea of fostering dogs would work out or if we'd made a horrible mistake by saying yes. In fact, there was no way of knowing back then if we made the right decision. When you first start out on a new journey there really is no way of knowing if it was the smart thing to do. You start to discover that after you've taken a few steps in that journey, after you've experienced a few things along the way, only then are you able to start putting things together in your head to come up with a sort of self-assessment of your idea. And it can be a scary proposition, can't it?

You have this idea you want to try out, but you're afraid you might fail. You're not sure if it's going to turn out the way you envisioned and you certainly don't want to look like a fool if the whole thing falls apart or worse, yet, turns tragic. And aren't they the feelings that stop us from doing something we dreamed of doing? Maybe not entirely these feelings, but they certainly play a role in our decision making (or lack thereof).

It's probably part of human nature that makes us not want anyone to see our efforts until we've mastered them. That's certainly the way we, in our culture, see our sports heroes: Sports channels don't have highlight reels filled with the hard work put in by these athletes, the reels are filled with unbelievable catches, fantastic goals, shots scored that didn't look like they had a chance of going in. And then we see the celebrations with teammates, peers of the hero hoisting him or her up on their shoulders as if they were the field general who just won the big battle. Sure, there might be a few clips of the hero in his or her younger years, quick snapshots of what they looked like growing up, or in high school or college. But you don't see an hour-long special of nothing but time spent in the gym or on the track, or at the physical therapist's office or with the trainer. That would make for some pretty boring television. So we focus on the end result—the big play, the grand finale, the winning play.

I don't think there's one competitor who wants to make the blooper highlights...

So we, you and me, join them in going through life not wanting to make the blooper reels, not wanting to be embarrassed or ashamed of what we decided to try. What would our lives *really* look like if we did try that one thing that we knew we couldn't fail at?

I don't think I'm alone in thinking there is one thing we can try where we don't have to worry about looking foolish. It's called hospitality. When we show hospitality to others, we open more than our front doors—we open our hearts. When we open our hearts without expectation of anything in return, we make the *Top 10 Plays of the Day*. It's when we open our hearts and expect something for it that we run the risk of making the blooper reels. Anyone will do something good if they expect a payday from it; even the most horrible people we can think of will do that. It takes someone who wants to really make a difference to open their heart and allow others to benefit instead of themselves.

In his book, *The 3 Promises*, bestselling author and TEDx speaker David Pollay talks about the difference between being a guest and being a host—of acting like a guest and acting like a host when we're around others. A guest, David says, stays back and watches what goes on. The guest doesn't start conversations or try to learn more about the others. But a host goes out of her way to make others feel welcome. A host wants to learn more about the guests and wants the guests to feel comfortable and at ease so they can enjoy themselves.

I hadn't looked at myself as either a guest or a host until I read *The 3 Promises*. But after reading it I realized that a lot of the times in my life I was a guest. I sat back and watched. Now I guess I could attribute (blame?) that on my years of being a cop. Cops tend to not want to draw attention to themselves in public and are always watching others, trying to maintain that tactical advantage that we're all taught in cop school…I mean, the police academy.

I'm going to go for a cheesy pun here: That would be a cop out! Sorry, it was an idea that just jumped in my head and I thought, "What's the worst that can happen if I share it?" Did I make the blooper reels with that one? Yeah, I probably did, didn't I?

Elissa can walk into a room with a bunch of people she's never met and by the time we're headed home, she knows all their names and a little bit about each one. Me? I'm still trying to remember the name of the host who threw the party. But that's not an excuse to not act like a host and open my heart to learn more about people by making them feel welcome, be it in my home or in my journey on planet Earth.

I wonder if dogs feel the same way? After watching all the butt sniffing that goes on in our house whenever a new foster dog arrives, I gotta think that dogs drop their guard a little quicker, and easier, than us humans. At least that's the way it's been with Bailey. The little ball of yellow fur we brought home from a farm years ago was asked to be a gracious host to every imaginable dog breed, temperament, and personality that we fostered. From Moe and Larry to Eliot, and every dog in between, not once did Bailey show anything other than excitement and joy. Here's the interesting part of her acceptance of other dogs: because I got sick within a year of bringing her home, we never really socialized her with other dogs. She was never to a dog park, and we rarely (if ever) had someone stop over our house who had a dog with them. Other than the occasional dog we'd pass on our walks, she never had the chance to play with another dog. Man, now that I read what I just typed, do I feel bad. I hope Bailey forgives me for not getting her out more than we did, and I hope we've made up for it with the opportunities we've given her to be the host.

I could see if she was brought up with other dogs around her how she might be so accepting and gracious. But she was like an only child being asked to share her toys. And her bedroom. And her parents. I'm amazed, and thrilled, that she made everyone who walked through our door feel welcomed. And what about that word, *welcome*? What does it mean to make someone feel welcome?

How many synonyms can you think of for the word welcome? I'm not talking about thesaurus words (but feel free to use one), I'm asking when you hear the word welcome, what comes to mind? I bet if we compared lists right now, we'd have an ideal way to treat people!

Bailey didn't need a thesaurus, she didn't need to Google the word to find out how she should act, and she didn't need to be told by us how to act. Not once. Somehow she just knew. Was it instinct? Was it an understanding that neither Elissa nor I were aware of? Or was it just the right thing to do because she didn't know any other way to act? She didn't just tolerate all the craziness that ensued, she embraced it. All of it. How many of us would tolerate having our lives turned upside down the way hers was? How many of us would embrace that idea?

When I was still ministering at the church I asked the kids: What's the difference between tolerating someone and embracing them? This was during one of our Sunday night youth group meetings where the topic of bullying was being discussed. I asked my teenage charges what it looks like when they tolerate their younger brothers or sisters. Oh, the answers they came up with! That was followed up with listing other things they were asked to tolerate in their young lives. That list included things like their mother's cooking, visiting a family member, having to watch the same TV show as their parents, and some of their teachers' quirkiness. When we looked at the list, they were asked if any of the things listed brought feelings of joy or happiness. Without exception, the answer was no. Nothing on the list that they had to tolerate made them happy or brought them joy.

If that's the case, why do schools preach tolerance in antibullying campaigns? If you and I are asked to *tolerate* each other, what does that convey? And what does it convey to our children? When used in that context, the word tolerate doesn't have a positive undertone, does it? And yet, we're told we need to tolerate each other in society, to tolerate our differences. When said like that, how can the one doing the tolerating not feel superior to the one being tolerated? Or the one *being* tolerated not feel inferior?

Getting back to my youth group, I asked them to replace the word *tolerate* with *embrace*, and then asked them how the other person would feel if instead of being tolerated, they felt embraced. I continued the discussion with the prospect of changing out the word tolerate, when it comes to our differences, with the word embrace. Now what do their young lives look like? What are the possibilities?

A wise friend of mine, Kevin Touhey, who happens to be a bestselling author himself, shared with me a little secret he uses. He told me to change out the word expectations with the word possibilities. Instead of expecting a certain number of people to show up at one of my talks, I should think of the possibilities of who might show up; instead of expecting my youth group to understand a concept I'm trying to present, I should think of the possibilities of what they might learn, and instead of expecting people to act a certain way because of the values I hold, I might want to consider the possibilities of what we might share with each other. In doing that I welcomed in a new way of seeing the world—and myself. Expectations have conditions and can lead to disappointment, possibilities are endless.

> Man is a dog's idea of what God should be.
>
> —Holbrook Jackson

Did Elissa and I expect Bailey to act a certain way, or did we think about what was possible? I wish I could give a definitive answer one way or the other. I'd like to think we considered all the possibilities, but I have to admit that we did have an expectation as well. I also have to wonder what Bailey thought of us, here we'd changed everything she understood as normal and replaced it with varying forms of chaos. Did she have expectations of us? Or did she just see possibilities in her life?

It's been said dogs live in the moment. They don't understand the concept of worrying about things in the future. What a gift! If Bailey was living in the moment each day we had a foster dog (or dogs) in our home, this girl has a lot to teach everyone. She didn't project her fears of how much heartache these ankle-biters might cause. And she didn't concern herself with how much pee or poop (and the occasional puke) would have to be cleaned up the next morning. All she knew was that today mattered. She wasn't about to trade time from the present to time in the future when she could live her day *today*. How many of us can say that?

And in living in the present she was the master of her domain. She was the queen among all the dogs, each and every one, that stayed in our house. Watching her explain the rules was more than entertaining, it was a lesson in life.

Bailey's first order of business for each new dog was to greet them, and she accomplished this with a wagging tail and ears up and alert. She wasn't about to wait to see if the other dogs liked her before she let them know that they were welcome, she let her body language do the talking by signaling that it was safe inside and she was there to help the newbies have fun.

Next up on her agenda was explaining the rules of the backyard. After the dogs were safely introduced and we were sure they were getting along on their initial walk, they went out back and ran. And ran. And ran some more. They played with toys, but mostly they played with branches and sticks lying about the yard. Bailey gave every dog an escorted tour around the perimeter of the fence as well as all the good hiding places toward the rear of the property. This was usually done not through a game of *follow the leader*, but instead the game of "See if you can catch me."

There was a method to our madness, why we allowed the dogs to run and play. It was to tire them out for their baths. And Bailey was more than willing to assist us in this endeavor. So as soon as Bailey got them tired out, she led them into the back door for their baths. Only Bailey knew this was coming and she couldn't wait! You'd think a dog might get tired of getting a bath, but not our

Bailey. She looked forward to each and every bath. And there was no way she'd let us get away with giving another dog a bath without including her. Elissa and I learned (quickly) that our window of time was narrow, it doesn't take that long for young dogs to get their second wind. That's why Elissa prepared the bathroom while they were outside running. Once they came back in, it was all business—the business of bathing. And once again, Bailey was eager to demonstrate for those not accustomed to the ritual of a bath at the Williams Canine Hotel. She was usually the first one in the shower and the last one out of the shower. As an added bonus, for puppies who didn't yet know how to shake their wet fur all over the bathroom, Bailey was more than willing to show them. As the two senior canine instructors who oversaw the scent class I was in with Boomer used to say when they saw a Labrador Retriever acting like, well, acting like a Labrador Retriever, "Labs!"

Dinnertime usually followed the baths and this was the hardest of things for Bailey to teach. She understood that in order to have her bowl placed in front of her, she had to sit. And until everyone was sitting, no one was getting fed. Well, she would sit right away, but the other dog(s) who were excited to get some vittles in their bellies didn't want to learn any rules at that moment. They wanted to eat. And the longer their bowls of food were held, the more frustrated they got. What Elissa couldn't communicate to the newest pack members, Bailey seemed to have little problem. A few well-placed barks in the direction of the jumping dogs and they stopped their antics just long enough for Elissa to get their attention back and have them start over. Sure Bailey probably got frustrated at them, but she never acted angrily toward them and she never snarled if they finished their dinner first and went over and stuck their noses in her bowl.

Playtime in the house was the next order of business and Bailey enjoyed showing everyone the ropes inside as much as she did in the backyard. The rules, according to Bailey, were simple: everyone had to get along. Whether it was an antler or a spot on the sofa, she wanted everyone to get along. The other rule had more to do with decorum than anything else. There was a certain level of rough-housing allowed, but Bailey set that limit and she was in control of keeping it. If a couple of the puppies began playing too rough, she'd run and bark while standing over them until they settled down to a decibel level more to her liking. Again, the barking was more of an attention getting sound than anything aggressive sounding.

Lastly, Bailey demonstrated how to go to bed. It was simple: Make sure you go to bed with an antler in case you feel like gnawing on something in the middle of the night.

> You don't own a dog, a dog owns you.
>
> —Unknown

Bailey mastered the rules—some of them ours, some hers. In doing so, she also mastered life. She mastered both her life *and* our lives. Dogs look to us humans as their masters, at least that's the way it was written up in the plans. That's the way it's supposed to work, in reality I wonder who is whose master.

I thought Bailey would know who her masters were as soon as we brought her home from that farm as a puppy. It didn't take long for all of us—Elissa, Matt, Corey, and me—to understand that she was allowing us to share her house. And I'd imagine that we weren't alone in that predicament. I've heard other dog owners talk about their dogs running their homes. Heck, my doctor tells me about his dogs (and cats) ruling his place. He's a well-respected specialist who has patients so loyal to him that we wait hours in order to see him. Can you imagine having an appointment at a scheduled time and you get there to see a waiting room filled with people who arrived hours before you got there. You've been there, haven't you? Now be honest, how upset did/do you get? Makes your blood boil too?

Here's what's unique about this doctor, no one complains as they sit there waiting for him, everyone knows what they'll get when they go back to see him. This doctor makes you feel like you're the only patient he has when he sees you. He shuts the door behind him and *he waits*. He waits for you to tell him about yourself and your family, he asks questions about your kids and what they're up to, then he asks about your goals and your hopes. And in between all that, he tells you about his family, his kids, and his hobbies. And his pets. He always tells you about the latest adventures of his dogs and cats. If you bring a spouse along, the conversation grows to find out how she's doing, and if your spouse is Elissa, you find yourself sitting there watching a conversation go on to include every topic under the sun.

For a moment you forget that you're in an examination room talking to a doctor. For a few minutes you feel as though you're getting caught up on things with an old friend. And it's only after the conversations about you and your goals and your hopes and your fears are over with that you get to talking about how you're feeling. You don't mention your pain or your ailments until you've finished talking about things that are seemingly mundane. After all the benign stuff is done and over with, that's when he gets to work on you. And for as long as you're in that room, you are the only thing that matters to him.

And that's why his patients wait to see him. We wait for hours and hours in that waiting room. We get to know one another because no one is pissed off that they have to wait. We understand that although he makes his appointments for a certain time, he immediately gets behind schedule as soon as he sees his first patient. And the delays snowball through the day until he's hours behind schedule. But that's okay with all of us who wait to see him. This doctor acts the part of a host. He welcomes you and treats you in a way that puts you at ease. His idea of hospitality is that which doesn't rush things, and he won't be rushed with his patients. He's mastered his trade in a way that doctors from all over refer their patients to him. So, as a patient, we wait. And we talk about pets, pets that allow us into *their* home.

Bailey doesn't know about time. It's been said that dogs have no concept of time. I'd imagine that if she had to wait in a room filled with strangers she'd make the best of it and act the part of the host. She would want to get to know you, probably by sniffing your crotch. Once you pushed her snout out from between your legs, you'd see that she wants to be your friend. Then you'd see her work the room, doing the same thing to everyone sitting there. Bailey would masterfully do her thing until everyone knew a little bit about her. And in doing so she would be demonstrating hospitality in a way that makes you feel like you're sitting in the front row, in that place of honor.

We humans like to believe that we are the masters of this planet. If that's the case, we need to understand a few things about ourselves and our role as master. How will we make others feel welcome? Can we see the possibility in others or will we expect certain things from them? And finally, how are we going to show hospitality in a way that isn't judgmental?

> Do not forget to show hospitality to strangers, for by so doing some people have shown hospitality to angels without knowing it. (Hebrews 13:2)

We have a responsibility to act the part of what a master needs to be in order to be both successful and compassionate. Our dogs, yours and mine, teach us by example what it means to be a master. They set an example for us not through their actions, but by our response to their actions. They allow us to act the role of master and then evaluate our response to their actions, to their playfulness, to their honest interaction with everyone they meet, and to their love.

If we claim to know a Divine Master then perhaps we need to act with a sense of humility of heart by allowing others to see how skillfully we've mastered our trades—trades of compassion, hospitality, putting others in the place of honor, and acting the host. Only then can we truly share the Good News of seeing the Divine in what we Master.

Bailey fetches the biggest sticks in the yard.

Bailey's enjoying a well-deserved rest.

Bella

...Grant that I may not so much seek
to be consoled, as to console...

One of the saddest days in the life of someone who fosters a dog is when that dog is adopted. One of the happiest days in the life of someone who fosters a dog is when that dog is adopted.

The adoption of a foster dog is a paradox where an end is a beginning, saying good-bye means saying hello; where joy brings tears to the eyes. After a person, or family, agrees to adopt, the days that dog is with its foster family pass by with mixed emotions. Days that once dragged on now seem to fly by in the blink of an eye. Memories flood your mind from the first day the dog walked into your home until that moment where you find yourself gazing at her, recalling all you've been through together. And it was *together*— neither of you got through the days on your own. You were part of her life and she was part of your life. And now, in just a few short days, things are going to be different for both of you.

You, as the human part of the partnership, worry about things that you have no control over. Worrying about her being accepted by her new family; will they understand all her quirks? You think about all the time you spent together; will she miss me? Your concern includes her emotional wellbeing; will she be happy?

The days tick off the calendar like the days left on your vacation. You find yourself dreading the last couple of days because you know that once that last day hits, it's all over. And that's the way it feels when you're a foster parent in a rescue organization as soon as you find out one of the dogs in your home is being adopted. It's bittersweet, just like that vacation you enjoyed; you're grateful for the time spent, but you know it can't last forever. It was never supposed to last forever. It was always going to be a temporary stint to enjoy something special.

There are a few adages out there about the preciousness of time, one of them is, "Make every second count." When the notification comes that one of your foster dogs is going, you realize just how true it is, and you wish you would've appreciated it a lot sooner. We humans are a funny species, aren't we? We can't wait to share all these nice sayings about life, and then it's as if we put them on a shelf until the last minute. You have to wonder what our lives would look like if we really did *make every second count.*

We either wait until we're literally saying good-bye to a loved one or we receive life-changing medical news before we see life as both precious and fragile. You'd think a guy who is ordained into the Christian ministry would practice what he preaches. You'd think...

Sure I preached it. With almost thirty years in the emergency service field, I've seen my share of death and dying, of pain and suffering. That should be enough to make anyone appreciate every moment, to make every second count. Shouldn't it? Like I said, I've preached it to the congregation; I am just a slow learner when it comes to practicing it. It wasn't until I received my own life-changing diagnosis that I fully grasped the idea that life really is a fragile gift. So allow me to offer some more free advice (remember my marital advice way back when?): Life is short, life is precious, and life is something that shouldn't be taken for granted; make time *now* for what and who you love. There's my public service announcement, I promise, no more preaching.

We now return to your regularly scheduled book reading.

It's times like these that you wish you didn't yell so much, that you weren't so critical of everything; you wish you could take some of the unkind words back. You wish you would've used a different tone of voice. If only you could go back and get a do-over. Oh, how I would make a promise to myself not to say some of the things I *did* say and to make sure I said a lot of things I *didn't* say. How about you? Any regrets along the way?

We're in good company, aren't we? I don't think any of this makes us bad people; I think it makes us human. We want to do the right thing, we want to appreciate every minute we're here on this planet, but there are issues that come up along the way. Like the pressures of a job or school, financial obligations, relationship issues, the needs of our family, and if we're lucky, maybe a few hours a week to find a hobby we enjoy. Sure we fail, but it doesn't mean we shouldn't keep trying.

> Sometimes the ones who have the brightest
> smiles have known and endured deep darkness.
> Knowing this, there is no reason I cannot
> survive my days with gloomy skies.
>
> —Dodinsky

As we appreciate life and realize that we're all human, we also need to acknowledge that we're prone to make mistakes and even make decisions that can harm another. Whether it's due to ignorance or just plain apathy, when we make decisions based on our own best interests instead of the best interests of those we've been asked to care for, there are resolutions that need to be made by those in charge.

Without going into details of what transpired, a family that had fostered dogs for our organization for some time was removed from the ranks because a dog in their care was left alone in a home without heat. Due to a powerful storm that hit the area, power outages were widespread and this family took refuge elsewhere until power could be restored the following day. However, that was one day too long for a dog to be left alone. Even though this dog had food and water and the family returned a couple of times to let it out, it was in the home alone all night long. So there really wasn't much of a decision to make.

We learned this right after the dog was adopted. The action taken was immediate. The dog's name was Bella and she was a loveable Lab mix—black with a white belly. That belly had black spots all over it. What really gave character to her looks was a white stripe that started at the front of her head and ran down her snout, which then widened as it dropped across the right side of her nose. She was as unique as her looks!

The family who adopted Bella had a toddler who was going to enjoy the companionship of his first dog. The love of a dog is something so special that I personally believe every child should have the opportunity to experience it. I know, I'm a little biased, but there's even research that suggests owning a pet has positive health benefits. I can still remember the first pet we had growing up, his name was Teddy and he was a medium-sized dog with white and black fur. My brother and I loved Teddy. But one day Teddy got loose and we were never able to find him. I'd like to think that someone found Teddy and gave him a loving home. The next dog that came into our home was from our aunt and uncle's farm in Hershey, Pennsylvania. I think our parents felt bad for my brother and me because we'd been pining about Teddy for years after he was gone. Our aunt and uncle had a couple of dogs and one of them, a Poodle mix, somehow got herself pregnant.

Our *Fluffy* was born on the farm and we brought her home as soon as she was weaned from her mother. Fluffy was nothing like Teddy. She was smaller than Teddy, much smaller. And the only resemblance she had to a Poodle was her curly hair. Matted hair is probably more accurate. What Fluffy lacked in beauty she made up for in affection. Fluffy loved everyone and it was this dog that my brother and I learned our dog-sitting techniques from. That's because both our parents worked and the responsibility to take care of Fluffy fell on us until they got home. We learned how to walk her, but not how to brush her. Her coat was just too tangled for us to attempt any kind of grooming. That task fell to our mom. Fluffy was with us all the way through our high school years. And it was during all those years that we learned how to care for a dog.

I still hold those memories dear to my heart, and it's those memories that keep me going when I get upset at things like what happened with the foster family that left Bella alone. Everyone was glad that Bella was going to a family that was going to give her love and protection, and provide comfort to her when a storm came instead of leaving her alone. We all want to find safety when storms hit, don't we? And for those who are scared, comfort is a priority. Bella would not only be given these most basic of needs, she would provide them as well.

Bella arrived in her new house with all the fanfare you'd expect in a loving home environment. Bella's new parents bought toys and treats as well as personalized food and water bowls. They were excited for her arrival in her new home, a small child waited anxiously at the living room window for his new puppy. You can picture it, can't you?

Bella received all the love she deserved. And as a bonus, she had a child to play with. From all accounts, this was a perfect match. A chief concern for any rescue is placing the right dog in the right home. The process to adopt is an intense one, for the main reason that each dog deserves the best home possible. I have to assume that there are some animal rescue organizations that are simply concerned with getting their dogs (and maybe cats, or in the case of our rescue, the occasional potbellied pig) adopted out. It certainly allows for more cash flow. But the reputable ones conduct some kind of background check and home visit before approving any adoption application.

The background check, including veterinary history, personal reference confirmation, and home visit were all conducted before Bella's adoption application was approved. And yet, a few days after she was adopted something went wrong. The family's son, the child who waited by the window for Bella to arrive, was found to be severely allergic to dogs. The family never had a dog before so there was no way for them to anticipate this diagnosis. They tried to work it out, but when they had to rush their son to the emergency room because of a severe asthma attack, they knew what they had to do.

We got the call late one afternoon and Matt and I headed over to the family's home. Their son was at a family member's house when we arrived. He wouldn't be able to come back until Bella was gone and the house was cleaned. I felt the sadness of the parents as they handed us Bella's food, her leash, a brand new collar that she wasn't quite big enough to fit into, food and water bowls with her name on them, chew toys, and two stuffed animals that she was fond of and kept with her in her crate.

Matt and I tried our best to console them. We wanted to make sure they knew that they did nothing wrong. In fact, finding out about their son's severe reaction now might have been the best thing because they witnessed it while they were home with him. Had they waited a couple more years to get a dog and neither parent was home when he had that reaction...

Bella was just as sweet as was reported to us by Taryn who brought her up to New Jersey in a transport from a shelter in Maryland a few months earlier. The foster family she went to reported that Bella was one of the sweetest dogs they ever had in their home. Once adopted, the family shared with everyone how sweet Bella was. Her picture was plastered all over Facebook as the family wanted to share the joy of their new arrival. Matt and I could see right away why this was such a sad time for the family. Some cynics might be tempted to say that there's no way a family can feel that close to a dog they've had only a couple of days. I would imagine those folks have never had the opportunity to feel the love of a dog. Without any hesitation, Bella followed Matt and me out the front door of the home and jumped in our car. Within fifteen minutes of pulling up to their house, Bella was on her way to her fourth home in as many months.

> I think dogs are the most amazing creatures;
> they give us unconditional love.
> For me they are the role model for being alive.
>
> —Gilda Radner

For all she had been through, Bella was calm and relaxed when she walked into our home. We would have understood if she was a little antsy or maybe even shy. After all, she never had a chance to plant her roots in any one place. What would our lives feel like if we'd been moved from place to place the way Bella was? Elissa and I, along with Matt and Corey, thought we'd have our hands full trying to socialize Bella as well as make her feel welcome. We felt it was our obligation to her.

What we quickly learned was that Bella was not only sweet and unbelievably well-adjusted, she was also smart. Bella was so smart that she ended up being the one who taught us about comforting others. As much as we wanted to comfort her, she let us know that she was okay and she wanted to be the one doing the comforting. She did this by her actions, not her words. She'd not just cuddle when Elissa was stressed about paper grading deadlines or getting her lesson plans done, Bella nudged her hand and laid her chin on Elissa's knee. No words were necessary and Elissa had no trouble reading what Bella was saying. Bella was telling Elissa to calm down and relax. Elissa doesn't know how to explain it any better than that; when she was stressed, Bella found her way next to her and made sure Elissa was distracted through petting the side of her neck or stroking the top of her head. Same thing with Matt and Corey, she'd go over to them when they seemed stressed and do whatever she could to distract them from whatever they were doing that was stressing them out. This wasn't always the best thing to do as some of Matt's and Corey's stress came from playing video games and any distraction to killing monsters or enemy bad guys ends in disaster for the player. Apparently both Matt and Corey had to explain to their teammates why they didn't cover them or why they weren't shooting any of the opponents that they said they would. I guess you really do need two hands to play those intense videogames.

When Bella saw me sitting in a chair or lying on the couch, she made sure to come over to me and see how I was doing. All the other dogs could be running and playing, Bella would only join them after she checked to see how I was doing. If I was having a bad day, she would stay with me—sometimes she would stay *on* me! It wasn't unusual for Bella to climb up on the couch with me or finagle a way to sit next to me in the chair.

It wasn't just humans Bella sought to comfort. There were a few days where Bailey wasn't herself, with vomiting and diarrhea. We didn't know what was wrong, but we knew something was going on. Instead of playing with the rest of the pack, Bella stayed with Bailey. She didn't crowd her, but it was obvious she was concerned and didn't want anything to do with the other dogs. Luckily, Bailey recovered without anything more than antibiotics prescribed by Dr. Cobb who came to our house on her way home from work. Even Dr. Cobb noted the gentleness of Bella who stayed near Bailey while she was examined. One has to wonder if Bella was staying near Bailey out of concern or to keep an eye on Dr. Cobb.

Dwight Moody tells the story of a blind man sitting on a busy street corner holding a lantern. A passerby walked up to him and asked why he had the lantern; after all, he was blind and the light was of no use to him. The blind man simply replied, "So that others won't stumble and can find their way." Have you ever met a person like the one Dwight Moody described? A person who puts the needs of others before herself?

I don't know about you, but the person I immediately thought of was my mom. She made sure my father, my brother, and I ate the best (usually the *un-burnt*) pieces of food at dinner. My mom was the most compassionate person I know, but cooking meals wasn't what she was known for. More than once we'd joke that she used the smoke detector as the kitchen timer. In most of her meals, at least one piece of whatever she was cooking was burnt. Each and every time that happened, she made sure that piece of dinner ended up on her plate, not ours. What she lacked in the kitchen, she made up for in love. And that meant she would comfort my brother and me before finding comfort for herself. If the house was cold (we didn't have much money growing up), she put the afghan she crocheted over my brother or me, not herself. If it was pouring rain and we had to get out of the car, she made sure my brother and I had the umbrella, not her. And if bad news hit our family, she would make sure everyone else was okay before she even tried to deal with the incident. In fact, when she was diagnosed with breast cancer, her first concern was how my brother and I would handle it, how her need for radiation and chemotherapy would impact *us*, not her.

Bella had that kind of personality, she made sure everyone, human and canine alike, were comfortable before she could feel at ease. That type of personality is a one of kind, to say the least. Her actions couldn't be taught, they were instinctive. Some might call it *intuitive*. Whatever it was, it made her special in the eyes of everyone who saw her. And there was one lady who saw her picture and read about her on Facebook. And this one lady couldn't help but ask to meet her.

> Piglet: *"How do you spell love?"*
> Pooh: *"You don't spell it, you feel it."*

Sharman is a local school teacher who taught both Matt and Corey. I was fortunate enough to get to know her when I was briefly assigned to the school where she taught. She's a determined and passionate teacher who expects the best from her students. Sharman completed the application and we set up an appointment for her to come over and meet Bella in person. I knew what was going to happen before she even arrived, but I played along like I wasn't sure if she'd like Bella.

I know why I was a little anxious waiting for Sharman to arrive at our home, it's because I always feel like a student whenever I'm around a teacher. I continue to look up to them for what they do and still don't want to disappoint them. I guess that goes back to my childhood and it was solidified when I witnessed what Elissa went through to prepare for each class. She taught three different courses and each one needed specific lesson plans. That's three separate lesson plans for each day of the school year. In New Jersey, students go to school 180 days a year. What's three times one-eighty? Hold on, let me get the calculator...

That's *a lot* of lesson plans! When you also consider the papers that need to be read and the tests that have to be graded, you quickly understand why teachers spend a lot of their off time doing school work. It's enlightening, isn't it? We really don't understand things as well as we think we do until we see them firsthand.

Another reason I still get a little anxious around teachers is because of our relationship throughout the years. Don't get me wrong, I love teachers (and I'm *in* love with a teacher), I just have certain memories of being sent to the principal's office. And each and every time it was a teacher who sent me there. My first trip "to the office" was when I was in third grade. What can I say, I wanted to get a head start on everyone else.

By the time I entered high school my parents were on a first name basis with each principal I had, and a few school board members as well. I wasn't officially suspended, however, until the first week of my freshman year of high school. Again, I wanted to get a head start on everyone else. When you do something that evacuates the entire school and gets the fire department dispatched, chances are you're going to get a few days off. In my defense, I was dared to do what I did in an electrical shop class. Luckily, I wasn't shocked or burned…

At least now you have some understanding as to why I was a little anxious awaiting a school teacher to show up at our door. Sharman was greeted at the front door by the entire pack, including Bella. And Bella didn't disappoint, she showed Sharman why everyone loved her. And Sharman knew right then and there that Bella was going to be hers.

Which brings us full circle to the opening of this chapter. Elissa and I, along with Matt and Corey, were thrilled that Bella was getting adopted by someone as caring and compassionate as Sharman. All of us knowing her made it even nicer. The problem would be saying good-bye. As much as we love seeing our foster dogs get adopted, we hate having to say good-bye. That's true of each and every dog we fostered; this good-bye was as bittersweet as they would come.

This was that paradox, where the saying good-bye for one is a saying hello for someone else. And certainly, where joy brings tears to the eyes. It was also a time to reflect on all that Bella taught us.

In this line of the Prayer of Saint Francis, the author is asking the Divine Master for strength or guidance or wisdom (maybe all three) that he "may not so much seek to be consoled, as to console." Put another way, instead of seeking to be comforted ourselves, that we might comfort another instead. Not an easy task when you think about how we humans seek comfort in times of distress. Now it certainly isn't hard to comfort another when they are in distress, that's a sign of compassion. But this is suggesting more than just comforting another, this is about comforting another when we ourselves also need comfort; when we ourselves are hurting and in need of a compassionate hug or kind word. There's the difference.

When I think of all Bella went through to reach the home of Sharman and her family, I'm dumbfounded by the fact, when considering everything that took place, she sought to comfort more than to be comforted. Bella actually sought out those in need and tried her best to console them, be they human or canine. Bella could very easily be that blind man sitting on a busy street corner holding a lantern for everyone else. Like the blind man, she was more concerned to see that others wouldn't stumble and to ensure that they found their way.

I'd imagine you and I can learn a lot from Bella, and dogs like her. We've all heard about a dog like this, we've read stories, or watched videos on the internet of a fascinating tale of a beloved canine companion. What happens after we close the book, or log off our computer? Does the story get absorbed? Do we take the lesson with us? And if we do, how long does it stay? The challenge isn't finding stories like Bella's; the challenge is keeping those stories alive in our hearts. We don't need to remember the details, we only have to recall the lesson: Our lives were made better because of those who sought to comfort us instead of finding their own comfort. People who made sure we had the piece of food that wasn't burnt, people who made sure we were warm and dry, people who made us feel safe at the risk of their own wellbeing, these are the people we remember.

And every now and then, we recall how we were made to feel by watching a pet teach us about life. Sharman and her family renamed Bella *Raven*, and I can't think of a name better suited for this wonderful creature. According to National Geographic, the Raven is an intelligent bird that gathers in flocks during the winter and at night, presumably for protection. They are believed to mate for life and both parents care for their young. The Raven, once almost brought to the point of extinction, can now be found from the icy Artic to the warm Mediterranean, as well as urban areas.

Like her namesake, Bella has adapted to a variety of climates and locales. She's been in places that were icy cold. But she ended up in a home filled with warmth. She was almost brought to the point of extinction, she was bounced from house to house, and she was asked to adjust each time she landed someplace new. But through it all, she never got her feathers ruffled; she maintained an air about her that said she was okay, that she had it all under control. And Bella made sure the flock she found herself in was warm and dry, and they felt protected. Every one of them.

Good News doesn't always travel through conventional means, sometimes it can be shared through the eyes of a dog.

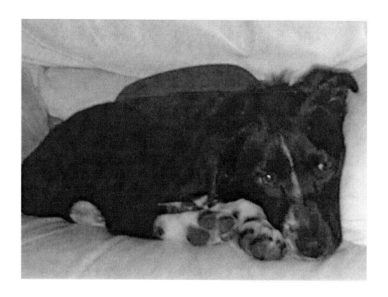

Bella enjoyed curling up on this
chair every day she was with us.

Klaus

...To be understood, as to understand...

Returning a dog because a child is severely allergic to it, such as in Bella's case, is one of those rare circumstances where a family has no choice. It's heart-wrenching and it's more of a rational decision than a choice. A rational decision is when you avoid the seafood bar because you're deathly allergic to shellfish; a choice is opting for the Caesar salad over the tossed salad.

A rational decision is based on need, not want. Returning a dog because of very real health risks is a rational decision. Returning a dog you bought your child as a Christmas present because it got too big *is not* a rational decision—it's a choice. And it's these kinds of choices people make with their pets that drive people who work with rescues out of their minds.

If you want to see something sad, visit your local shelter anywhere from the end of February through April. This is the time frame when shelters start receiving unwanted Christmas presents, pets that were cute as kittens or puppies on December 25th, but lost their cuteness as they became bigger and more destructive. Parents who thought their young children would enjoy that doggie they picked out in early December learned that kids that age aren't going to take care of a pet no matter how much they promise. All the walks that the twelve-year-old said he'd take care of had a lot less priority than his friend's new PlayStation game. "I'll walk him when I get home" became the plea as he was running out the door. All the poop that the adolescent daughter promised to pick up in the yard quickly overwhelmed her and she lost interest in all but the fun things to do with her new puppy.

And the parents found themselves having less and less patience until one day...

Until one day they made a *choice*, they saw that this Christmas gift really wasn't working out and it was time to say good-bye. They chose to get rid of something that wasn't working out instead of devoting more time to it, instead of demonstrating to their children that hard work and perseverance pay dividends in the end.

That one day usually arrives two to three months after the gift is given. So anytime between the end of February through April is a good bet that you'll find returned Christmas presents sitting in cages in shelters across the country. And it's through no fault of the dog that she ends up in a cage instead of a warm family home; she wasn't part of the decision to be born. She wasn't part of the decision to be purchased as a gift. And she sure as hell didn't have any role in the *choice* to get rid of her.

I'm sorry, I just realized that I promised no more preaching. I think this was venting, maybe even ranting. Either way, I am sorry. Sometimes I just don't get it and my thoughts spill out onto these pages. I'll try not to let it happen anymore. Promise. No crossies this time!

You know what, we have to lighten this up a bit. Even I'm getting depressed by what I just wrote! So how about a question to lighten the mood? Here goes: If you give a boomerang as a gift and it's returned, does that mean the person didn't like it?

There, now we're back where we belong. Nothing like a good joke to lighten things up. Okay, you didn't care for it that much? A little too cheesy for your taste? Fine, you come up with a better one. I'll wait…

> You must not lose faith in humanity.
> Humanity is an ocean; if a few drops of the
> ocean are dirty, the ocean does not become dirty.
>
> —Gandhi

It was a Sunday afternoon when Klaus arrived in our driveway. Klaus was a little more than five months old and his family brought all of his favorite toys along with him. For as big of a puppy as he was, Klaus wasn't that sure of himself. We'd fostered dogs less than half his size who arrived at our house with more self-confidence than Klaus. His head hung low as his mom explained to us that he "just got too big for their family." She and her husband didn't know he would get that big and she said it was a really tough decision to let him go. Her daughters were upset by their decision, she told me; however, even though they were in the car that was idling in our driveway, they were never given the opportunity to say good-bye to their Christmas present. Their mom handed me the leash, got in the car, and left. Four little eyes belonging to two precious faces were staring out the back window as their mother drove off.

And just like that, we were the recipients of a returned Christmas gift. Maybe if I'd seen the way the girls interacted with Klaus I would've had a better understanding as to why he seemed listless. Maybe he just knew; maybe he knew his only crime was growing. I'd like to think that he had no idea and just thought he was at a new home that would show him the love he deserved.

Even though Klaus was purchased as a Christmas present, he wasn't a full-bred dog. We tend to think puppy mills only deal with full-breeds, but where there is money to be made, well—there is money to be made. Klaus was a mix of three dogs: Rottweiler, Shepherd, and Labrador Retriever. You should've seen the size of his paws! This was a big puppy and he was going to grow into a big boy.

We had hoped that Bailey would do her thing and bring Klaus out of his shell as she did with all the other dogs we'd fostered. While Klaus showed he was a quick study and learned all her rules of the house, he didn't get that gleam in his eyes that would show he was starting to feel at home. He reminded me of our first day with Dakota and I hoped I wouldn't have to spend another hour on the cold ground out back.

Instead of heading out back in the late winter air, we opted to let it go and just observe for a little while. What we witnessed was a room full of dogs bringing Klaus peace offerings, presumably to get him to see they wanted him there. He barely looked any of them in the eye. The other dogs were interested in how he smelled, but he showed no interest in sniffing their butts in return (I can't say I blamed him on that one).

Although Klaus didn't seem to be happy in our home, that didn't mean he wasn't hungry. Man, this dog could eat! Watching him eat put a smile on Elissa's face, she gets a special sense of satisfaction when she sees people enjoying her cooking. And she gets even happier if you ask for seconds. I tried to make her happy from the first day of our marriage, so I'd ask for seconds as often as I could. You want to know who this didn't make happy? My doctor! Less than a year into our marriage and I discovered I gained more than ten pounds. The good doc told me to lay off the pasta; Elissa called that advice sacrilege. I'm happy to report that I was able to find a happy medium and the weight's down quite a bit. Would you believe that now my problem is maintaining weight? Sometimes a guy just can't win.

Okay, Klaus was eating so chances were he wasn't sick. It must be in his head. So this should be easy, right? All we needed was a dog psychologist and we'd be in business. Since we didn't have one of those folks handy, we settled for the next best thing: going for a walk. Alone. Whenever we'd go on walk, each one of us would take a dog, or two. Very rarely did a dog go on a long walk by just itself. So after Elissa got the other dogs out the back door, I took Klaus and got his leash hooked to his collar. As soon as I opened the door he backed up and dug in like I've never seen. He *did not* want to go out that door.

> I used to look at [my dog] Smokey and think,
> "If you were a little smarter you could
> tell me what you were thinking,"
> and he'd look at me like he was saying,
> "If you were a little smarter, I wouldn't have to."
>
> —Fred Jungclaus

Okay, now I really needed a canine psychologist. What was going on with him? He ran out the back door with no hesitation, why was the front door so scary to him? The more I pulled on the leash, the more he pulled in the other direction. I stopped pulling after I saw how upset he was getting. So much for Plan B.

Later that night I noticed that Klaus wouldn't go anywhere near the front door, he'd make a wide arc around the entire entryway. And if he could avoid it all together, he would take that route; instead of walking past the door to go down the hall he'd go in the other direction through the dining room. For reasons unknown to us, Klaus wanted no part of the front door. I guess if I wanted to take him on walks of any kind we'd have to leave out the back door.

Except that now he didn't even allow the leash to be attached. There was something negative that he was connecting to whatever we were doing, and whatever we were doing wasn't working. This went on for days, although it seemed more like weeks or months. One afternoon our next door neighbor's daughter asked if she could say hi to the dogs. Gabby is a sweet nine-year-old who loved to say hi to the new dogs that arrived at our home. I explained to Gabby how Klaus was a gift from Santa but he got too big for his home, so his family asked us to take care of him until another family adopted him. Gabby replied that Klaus must've been scared when he got here. I shared with her how scared Klaus looked when he came out of his car in our driveway and how he looked walking into our door to meet everyone. With that, Gabby said, "I bet he doesn't want to go anywhere near that door or your driveway." I couldn't believe how she could know this. So I asked her, "Gabby, how did you know that?" And that's when she said that he's probably sacred that he's going to be taken to another home where he doesn't know anyone. She continued, "If I was Klaus I would want to stay right here inside where I knew I was safe. I wouldn't want anyone to take me away."

Out of the mouth of babes...

Almost one full week of trying to figure out what was going on with Klaus and all it took was a small child to see the world the way

Klaus saw it. All it took was a small child to have an open mind in order to understand how Klaus must be feeling. And all it took was a couple of adults to see the world the way a nine-year-old does. And it was a lot cheaper than a doggie psychologist!

Am I the only one who finds wonder in the wisdom of children? When I look back and think of the times I *hushed* my own children when they were trying to tell me something, I'm ashamed not only at the way I treated them, but at how many painful things I might have been spared if I only listened to them. Sometimes those of us who think we know the most need to ask for forgiveness the most.

With an understanding of the problem, we could now address it in a way that helped the situation instead of making it worse. One of our dear friends is a dog behavior specialist and we value her opinion and expertise. One of the things I'll always remember Christine telling me is that a dog's life goes by so much faster than ours, what is slow to us is fast to a dog. That's why it's important to not only have patience with a dog, but to move slowly as well.

With that in mind, we got to work. The first thing we needed to accomplish was getting Klaus to feel comfortable by the door. To do this I attached his leash to him and just let him be. The hardest part of this initial step was convincing the rest of the pack that we weren't going for a walk. I don't know what it's like at your house, but when the leashes come out in ours, the pack wants to get moving. We ended up attaching leashes to all the dogs and let them work out their disappointment on their own. Eventually they forgot the leashes were attached and they went about their usual business.

In order to get Klaus to trust me I'd grab his leash and walk around the kitchen, the room the farthest away from the front door. I'd praise him when he walked alongside me and then gave him a little treat when he sat. Next up, walking around the house. Slowly. Walking. Around. The house. Each time we got a little closer to the front door. When Klaus acted scared we'd stop and move back a step or two. He let me know where his comfort zone was. And I let him know it was okay and I wasn't going to push it until he was ready. And every time he calmed down at the edge of the imaginary line that he felt was his comfort zone, he was praised.

It was a two-steps-forward, one-step-back process, but eventually we were able to walk past the front door with very little anxiety on his part. I knew we passed the first hurdle when I let him run around (with the leash attached) and then call him to me. I'd position myself in the living room and he had no choice but to walk past the front door to get to me. His reward—another little treat.

The next hurdle was to get him to look out the door. To do this we put all the dogs out back and then I opened the front door, with the full-length glass storm door being the only thing between the inside and the front porch. We called the dogs back inside and let them run around. Klaus never even noticed that the front door was wide open. My goal was to get Klaus to sit at the front door while being able to look out the storm door. "Slow is fast," I heard in my head. Christine knew what she was talking about. I worked for her for a short period of time and watched in amazement how she handled dogs that other trainers had given up on. Not only does she have no fear of any dog, she has a personality with them that says, "I'm in charge. Everything will be okay, but I'm in charge." So when I heard her voice in my head, I knew I better listen. We worked slowly, I didn't want him to think I was tricking him into something he didn't want to do. He was going to do this because he was going to know that it was okay. It took a while and it was literally two steps forward, one step back. But we eventually made it to the front door and had Klaus sitting there, calm and relaxed as if he didn't have a care in the world.

I can't explain how it happened or exactly when it happened, but during our time together Klaus and I bonded. There was a sense of trust—in both directions. Klaus trusted me and I trusted Klaus. And that trust was based on mutual understanding of each other. Klaus needed to understand what I expected of him and I needed to understand how Klaus saw the world. Once we figured that out together, we had it made. Because shortly after Klaus was sitting at the front door (eating training treats that I fed him from my pocket), we were out the front door and in the front yard. Then we were out in the street taking a walk together. And then, we were gone, out of sight from the house and taking in the sights and sounds—and smells—of the neighborhood. We were gone for more than a half an hour and when we came back home, Klaus was welcomed by the rest of the pack who were waiting by the door. And it was then that I saw the gleam in Klaus's eyes. Klaus was home. Klaus was home safe and sound. And he knew it.

> We have two ears and one mouth so
> we can listen twice as much as we speak.
>
> —Epictetus

I've been told, more than once, that I'm a slow learner. I have to admit something to all those folks who accused me of that: You were right! But you want to know something? Klaus reminded me that slow is okay. Klaus basically told me to slow down and take it easy, there's no need to rush things. It'll all come to you at the right time. How did Klaus tell me this? How did he remind me? It was through the voice of a little girl who wandered over to our house one afternoon when both Elissa and I were at our wits' end trying to figure out what was wrong with Klaus.

Whenever we meet people where they are, on their terms, we're basically saying to them, "I'm interested in what you have to say." There aren't that many of us who aren't familiar with someone who dominates a conversation. You know who I'm talking about, don't you? The person(s) you have in mind and the one(s) I have in mind make sure you know everything about them, they can't wait to tell you as much as they can. Often as fast as they can. They don't seem very interested in you, do they? They're more interested in you being interested in what they have to say. And if you're at a gathering, you watch this person work the room going from group to group, sharing the same things you heard. And you're left to wonder if the person really cares about you or your life.

I was fortunate to know a man who was the entertainment editor for a syndicated newspaper. Whenever I saw Lou at gatherings he made sure to come over to me and start a conversation. As soon as he started the conversation, Lou closed his mouth and listened. He maintained eye contact and kept listening. And when I was done sharing a thought, Lou asked me to share more about it. He probed deeper to learn more about what I was talking about. He didn't try to figure me out, he just listened with a sense of interest. It was more than just paying attention, it was what some experts call *empathetic listening*. Using empathy while listening to a person share something with you takes practice. It means you put yourself in their shoes as they're talking, as if you are with them and the story being told is being told with you and about you—as if you are the person doing the talking. You don't just see it their way, you experience it the way that person experienced it.

That's what Lou did, not just with me, but with everyone he interacted with. He wasn't as interested in you learning about him and his week, rather he wanted to know about you and what you did that week. Or month. Or even last year. Lou didn't rush the conversation and he didn't force the topic, he wanted to understand what you were saying, he wanted to understand you. And when you walked away from that conversation you felt as if your life meant something, you felt as though a person who'd interviewed the stars of Hollywood was interested in your life and wanted to be a part of it. That is a gift; Lou enjoyed sharing it.

We all want to be understood, it's one of our needs. Relationships fail because one spouse believes the other *doesn't understand him/her.*

"He doesn't understand me."

"She doesn't understand how important this is to me."

"I'll never understand my kids."

"My parents don't understand me."

I'd imagine you can add a few of your own to that list. If all of us have a need to be understood, and that's the goal in all of our communication, who's doing the understanding? If folks in a relationship are only worried about being understood instead of understanding, is it any wonder relationships fail at the rate they do? And I'm not just talking about partnerships between adults, this disconnect is also between parent and child. You have to wonder if anything is going to change if we don't change the way we go about communicating.

A bad conversation is just a game of waiting for the other person to stop talking so you can talk about what you want that person to hear. But if we make the effort to understand someone at their level, on *their* terms, we have a much better chance to see the world through their eyes. So many times we try to understand a person on our terms, to, in a very twisted way, insist that they see things *our* way so we can understand *them*. It was what Elissa and I were doing with Klaus.

In German, the name Klaus means "Victorious People." If we're to have any chance at being victorious in the game of understanding, we first have to see ourselves as our most brutal opponent. It wasn't until we saw how wrong we were in our approach that we were able to help Klaus become what he was supposed to be—a happy, well-adjusted dog who loves being alive. Had we insisted on seeing things through our lens, frustration would have led to anger, and then resentment. And before you know it, any chance of developing a bond would have been gone.

It took the combined efforts of a dog behavior specialist and little girl to open my eyes and remind me that by taking my time, both Klaus and I would develop an understanding of each other and what we were struggling with. That understanding led to a desire to learn more, I wanted to learn more about Klaus and what he had to offer the world, and I'm sure Klaus wanted to learn more about me so he could trust and just live in the moment. Can you imagine what our lives would look like if we just took a page from what Christine, Klaus and Gabby taught me?

- Take your time

- See it from their perspective

- Be patient
- Have a desire to learn about the other person
- Listen with an empathetic ear
- Ask follow-up questions
- Be willing to admit you don't know everything

Does this list look like a summary of a yearning to understand more than being understood? It's been said that you can't understand someone while you're talking. The next time you have the chance, try listening with an empathetic ear. Be patient with that person who might need a little more time in order to be understood. Don't rush the conversation, take your time. Make it a point to learn something about the person that you didn't know before you started talking. Give it a go. What do you have to lose?

As we move forward in our own journey, we have opportunities to make a difference. Some of us will make a difference in the life of a child, others in the life of someone living alone. Maybe we'll make a difference in the environment, or in our work place. Even more of us will make a difference at our place of worship or a community initiative. And there are those who will make a difference in the lives of forgotten animals.

It feels good when we make a difference. It feels even better when we have an understanding of the cause we're working toward. And the only way to gain that understanding is to listen in a way that says I want to hear you more than I want to be heard. We need to see in a way that shows others we want to see what's in them instead of wanting others to take a look at us. And we need to seek to understand more than we seek to be understood. If we can accomplish this we just might be victorious people in ways we never could have imagined.

This desire to understand isn't just Good News for you and me, it's Good News for those in our lives as well.

Klaus took a liking to the same chair Bella loved.

Rocky, Part II

There could be worse things than being call a loser, right? I mean, our skin isn't so thin that being a called a loser is going to ruin our day, is it? Look, I was a cop for twenty-five years, I was called all kinds of things, so I was happy when someone remembered to use *all five* fingers when they waved to me! Still, nobody wants to be considered a loser, we all want to be winners.

When you see yourself as being successful in life, you stand a little taller, you walk with a little more confidence, and you feel good about yourself. You feel like a winner. And everybody loves a winner. If that's all true, than the idea of being loved should come easily to winners. Winners love to be loved. Just watch the postgame show of your favorite team. When they win, the fans go nuts and shower the team members with love. But when the team loses... Oh, when the team loses. I'm writing from the Philadelphia sports market, when one of our teams lose, it's not a pretty sight. Winners catch all the breaks and go far in life, losers aren't expected to go very far and they get none of the breaks. In fact, when you feel like a loser, the only luck you seem to have is bad luck.

As shared in previous chapters, Elissa and I had dogs come into our homes that other people saw as losers. These owners committed what may be the most unloving act of all in the eyes of a pet: They dropped their pets off at a shelter with no way of knowing what their future would be. However, what everyone who does surrender a pet *has to know* is that unless their discarded pet is adopted, they *will* be put to sleep. I can't think of an act, in the eyes of an animal, that's less loving than that.

When Elissa and I signed on to this cause, we promised ourselves that no matter what, each and every dog that came into our home would feel loved. We knew where these dogs would be coming from, we knew at least one human in their life felt they weren't worth keeping. And we couldn't imagine how that must have felt, to be dropped off in a cold, strange place, wondering if you'd ever see your owner again. We worried that these dogs might not trust us. Who could blame them? The last human contact they had abandoned them; would they be wrong to not trust another human ever again?

We knew there would be a lot of pee, we knew there would be a lot of poop, we were advised there would be heartache, and we hoped there would be love. This is a chapter about love, the kind of love you find in the eyes of a dog that's been rescued from a shelter. This is a chapter about the love you find in the heart of a dog who was once seen as worthless. And finally, this is a chapter about the failure of love, and the love of failure.

If you've been following along, you're aware that we've had a *pack* in our home during the fostering of a variety of the dogs already mentioned. And if you've kept up on the story, you know that the only dog I mentioned as being ours was Bailey, our yellow Lab. You can't have a pack of *dog*, you need more than one dog for it to be considered a pack. So where did the other dogs needed to make up a pack come from? I'll give ya a hint, we were (and still are) failures! I was told it happens to everyone in rescue programs, sooner or later everyone in an animal rescue fails. And we were no exception.

I guess I need to go back and start at the beginning, at least the beginning of where our failures began. He'd been with us for a little more than a month when an application came in on him. We'd fostered a bunch of dogs before this guy, so we should have expected this day would come. We did expect it, we just weren't prepared for it.

There was something about this one that melted our hearts, and not in a gooey, mushy way. This melting was the kind that says, "I understand." The message he conveyed was that he was mature enough to understand the craziness that was our home, and he was okay with it. He signaled to Elissa and me something neither one of us could articulate, and yet it was something both of us felt. Independent of each other's thoughts or feelings, the day the application came in we told one another that we had to talk. And, guys, you know that feeling when your wife tells you that there's something she needs to talk to you about. That one sentence has led to many a sleepless night for husbands all over the world!

But I had something I needed to share with her as well so we sat down to talk about what was on our minds. It was there, over a cup of coffee, that we talked about it. Elissa felt it and I felt it, whatever *it* was. It ended up being the feeling that neither one of us believed we could let Rocky go. Both of us had the same feeling, at the same time. That is, what some call synchronicity. And we believed if we both felt the same thing, at the same time, maybe we should listen to whatever the universe was trying to tell us.

We didn't know who the application was from, we knew nothing about the family that wanted to adopt Rocky. And it wasn't like we didn't care. We did care and part of us felt bad that we were denying a loving home the chance to experience what Rocky had to offer, especially his love. But we also knew that we would offer him love like no one else, we'd been doing that all along. Without us knowing it as it was happening, we had fallen in love with Rocky. It wasn't until we learned that he'd be leaving that we realized just how much we'd fallen for him.

We didn't have a lot of time to discuss our feelings, Taryn needed to know right away so she could tell the applicant that either Rocky was still available for an appointment to meet him or that he had been adopted. Before Taryn got that last word, adopted, out of her mouth, I told her that Rocky wasn't going anywhere. I thought Taryn would be upset by our decision, I thought we disappointed her. We were a foster family and our role was to love them temporarily until they were adopted by a family that would love them forever. Instead of being upset, Taryn laughed and said, "Welcome to the club!" She also shared with me that she had a feeling that we were going to fail with Rocky. She said she heard it in our voices when we spoke on the phone. From the day he arrived until that phone call, Taryn and I talked on the phone regularly and her experience told her that my words conveyed something that she heard in every other foster family who failed: I lost a sense of objectivity. I stopped talking about Rocky with any sense of detachment. Instead I began talking about him as if he was ours. And here I thought I was doing a pretty good job of hiding my feelings…

> Dogs have a way of finding the people who need them…
> filling an emptiness we didn't
> even know we had.
>
> —Thom Jones

It would be nearly impossible to describe the sense of relief we felt after we made this decision. How do you put into words something so deep and so passionate that you barely understand it yourself? It would be like trying to describe the smell of the letter G. Go ahead, see if you can do it. It means something different to everyone and trying to explain it is worthless. That's how it felt the day Elissa and I decided to adopt Rocky ourselves. It was a mix of emotions that included relief, joy, passion, elation, and love.

Love, that emotion that leads man to do some pretty amazing, and crazy, things. Like adopting a dog that you never had any intention of adopting when you started out. If it's hard to describe our feelings, it was just as hard for everyone else who met Rocky. As a foster family, you have to open up your house to others who will come to meet the dogs. When an application for adoption is approved, the person (or family) sets up an appointment to visit with the dog in your home. It's the first time that they'll meet the dog who they only know from a picture they saw on an internet site.

This is the time in any foster home where you hope your pack is on their best behavior. First impressions are important! More than once Elissa and I were embarrassed by the antics of one or more of the dogs who weren't being considered for adoption, but nonetheless made a point to make their presence known. I can't say if any of those incidents turned a potential adopter away, but they sure made things interesting.

Without exception, each and every family that came to our home to meet a dog they put an application on, asked if Rocky was available for adoption. And each and every friend or family member who visited and met him, asked if he was one of the dogs available to be adopted. Elissa and I would constantly joke with anyone who came over that they had to leave with a dog! It was our not so subtle way of doing our part to get the dogs adopted. To a person, they declined our offer to take a foster dog home with them, but they said if Rocky was available, they would take him. Everyone felt something when they met him. They might not have been able to articulate it, but they felt *it*. All those comments and inquiries about Rocky only solidified the affirmation we already felt and we had (have) no regrets. We know we made the right decision.

One of the first things we needed to do now that he was ours was to make an appointment for him with Dr. Cobb. The sending shelter advised our organization that Rocky was about ten months old. When Dr. Cobb examined him, she said he was well past ten months old, she could tell by his teeth. There were no puppy teeth left in his mouth and the teeth he did have were solidly planted and had been there a while—this as evidenced by the amount of tartar that had built up on them.

Here we thought we knew his approximate age and we were wrong. How wrong were we? How far off was the estimate the sending shelter made? By at least two or three years. That was Dr. Cobb's best guess, and she cautioned us that that's all it was, a best guess. With absolutely no record to go on, we were guessing about a lot of things. But overall, Rocky was in great physical shape and after a couple vaccinations, we were out the door and on our way home with our new three-year-old dog. Since we didn't have a clue when his real birthday was, we decided that his new birthday would be the day we adopted him!

We were now a family with two dogs of our own. That meant Bailey now had an assistant for her job in new dog orientation at the Williams Canine Hotel. But what would Rocky's role be? What was he good at? For all the time he'd been with us, we didn't really notice any demonstrative activity that established him as having any certain skill set. As it played out, Rocky's role was to be the voice of reason, he maintained calm. Just by his presence alone, Rocky set a tone that expressed what we as a family needed: A sense of calm. Where Bailey intervened, Rocky stood back and watched.

> Love is not an emotion. Love is a promise.
> —The Doctor, in the BBC series *Doctor Who*

Another attribute Rocky had was his ability to forgive. And that was much needed after I screwed up one afternoon while Elissa was out shopping. With her gone, I had a chance to arrange a few things in the garage, along the bench that ran across the back wall of the garage. It's one of the few tasks she still lets me tinker with. Since I was working in the garage, I let the dogs out the rear garage door into a small fenced-in area and kept an eye on them as I did my thing. No more than five minutes went by that I realized there was no more cleaner left to wipe down the top of the work bench. So I called them all back inside through the interior garage door and shut the door. Once they were inside the house, I grabbed my jacket and keys and headed out the door to run to the local hardware store. Since I would still be working in the garage when I returned, I left the overhead door open.

I wasn't gone more than fifteen minutes when I returned to the most heart-stopping sight imaginable: Rocky sitting in the middle of the flower bed in the front yard! He was sitting there, in between a few clumps of decorative grass that we planted the year before. I got out of my Jeep and called him over to me, he didn't move. I wasn't sure if he was mad at me or frightened. It wasn't until I started to walk toward him that he ran up to me and jumped all over me as I got down on one knee and asked him, "What are you doing out here?" I wasn't expecting an answer, but it sure would have been nice to know what he was thinking.

Once I got inside the house I realized what I had done—or, in this case, not done. I didn't count all the dogs before I left for the store. I forgot to make sure all the dogs came inside when I called them in the garage. In my haste to get what I needed at the hardware store, I made an assumption that all the dogs were in. How could I have been so careless? I still look back and think of what I would have done to myself if something happened to Rocky. What if he ran away and never came back, like Teddy did when my brother and I were kids? The thoughts made me sick to my stomach.

If Rocky could talk, I'd like to think that he would tell me he forgives me. I'd like to imagine a dog that loves me that much. The truth is I don't know what he would tell me. Maybe he would call me an idiot and hold a grudge. I wouldn't blame him if he did. But he didn't. He either forgave me or didn't think anything else of it after our reunion in the front yard. I had to wonder, *would I be that gracious?*

Not only did Rocky act as if it was no big deal, he flourished and grew in the days, weeks, and months that followed. Could it be that he was simply appreciative that I came back for him? Is it possible that dogs don't have a concept of resentment or evil, and therefore Rocky couldn't imagine me doing anything that would purposely hurt him or put him in danger? I have to wonder how much different our lives would be if we forgave that quickly. What would our relationships be like if we loved that deeply?

A trait of a dog that we hear over and over again is that they give unconditional love. If nothing else, the way Rocky dealt with me (compared to the way a human might) serves as an example of unconditional love—love without any condition whatsoever. We'd all like to be loved that way, wouldn't we? In fact, I bet there are more than a few of us who believe we deserve to be loved like that.

Can you imagine how that would feel? What would it be like to not worry if the person who loves you will never stop loving you, forever? No matter what you did, the person loving you will keep loving you the same way. Forever.

Yeah, I could live with that. And I'll go one better, I think that's the way I love, unconditionally. You too? Good for us, right? We love because that's the kind of good people we are, we needn't go any further.

"Are you sure that's the way you love, Rusty?"

"Who's that?"

"It's me, your conscience, Rusty. I'm that voice inside your head."

"Hey, I don't have to explain anything to you! I'm a good lover, just ask my wife."

Elissa, can you come here a minute?

You and me, we think we got it going on and we're not going to let some voice inside our heads tell us anything different! Are we?

Well, I'm not going to speak for you, but I will take this opportunity to throw myself on the sword and admit that maybe I don't always love unconditionally. I love unconditionally most of the time, just not all the time.

Since I'm being honest, I should probably admit that I don't love unconditionally most of the time, but I do love unconditionally a lot of the time. Okay, how about this; it's about as honest as I can be: I want to love unconditionally, I strive to be the kind of person who loves unconditionally.

Maybe we use that term too loosely, maybe it should really be saved for when we can back it up. I tell anyone who'll listen that I love my children unconditionally; I tell everyone that I love my bride unconditionally. The problem is, I'm not so sure I fully comprehend what that means. I know I've preached about the kind of love mentioned a bunch of chapters ago, *agape love*. Agape love is the Greek translation of the love the Apostle Paul used when he wrote the verses that have been read at countless weddings, that letter to the folks in Corinth where he talks about what *love is*.

Let me remind you how it goes. Here's the list, the way it's usually read:

Love is patient
Love is kind
[Love] does not envy
[Love] does not boast
[Love] is not proud
[Love] does not dishonor others
[Love] is not self-seeking
[Love] is not easily angered
[Love] keeps no record of wrongs
Love does not delight in evil, but rejoices with the truth
[Love] always protects
[Love] always trusts
[Love] always hopes
[Love] always perseveres
Love never fails

Now that's a list, wouldn't you agree? I adapted this list from 1 Corinthians 13:4–8. The actual passage reads like this: "Love is patient, love is kind. It does not envy, it does not boast, it is not proud. It does not dishonor others, it is not self-seeking, it is not easily angered, it keeps no record of wrongs. Love does not delight in evil but rejoices with the truth. It always protects, always trusts, always hopes, always perseveres. Love never fails."

When you go back and look at that list of how Paul described love, I think you'd agree that it represents, if nothing else, a form of unconditional love. And it's a fairly extensive list, wouldn't you agree? If this list represents the best in unconditional love, how do you think I stack up against it? Let me help you, not very well.

Let's start at the top. Am I patient? Well, some of the time I am, not as often as I'd like to be. Am I always patient with Elissa? Was I always patient with Matt and Corey when they were growing up? I'm afraid the answer is no.

Am I kind? I'd like to think I am. Do I act with kindness all the time? Am I kind to a person who's a jerk? Do I answer Elissa kindly when we're arguing? Nope, nope, and...no.

And we can go right on down the list: Of course I'm not envious of anyone or anything; I never boast (I'm the best at that, by the way); I wouldn't think of acting with foolish pride. Need I continue?

I'm not suggesting you hold yourself against this standard that I just did. No one could possibly act that way *all of the time*. But that doesn't mean we can't strive for it, there's no reason to not try to be the most loving person we can be. To give love more than we seek love. Did you notice in that list that nowhere is there a reference to how the writer is made to feel about love? Did you notice it was about the other person, the one being loved?

That, my friends, is unconditional love. As long as I'm feeling good and no one ticks me off, I can act that way all day long. But what happens when I feel lousy, or something affects my day that sucks the joy out of it? How apt am I to act in a way that I could go down that list and check off each quality? Not very likely.

I know I'm supposed to act that way, in fact, I've been *called* to act that way. You know, the *answering a calling* thing ministers do? Why is it that I can't get through that list on any given day of the week? Maybe because I'm human? You?

It does you and me no good to beat ourselves up for falling short. The best we can do is keep doing the best we can do and make today better than yesterday. Some people call that growth. And instead of getting down or wishing we were something we're not, we can continue putting one foot in front of the other and being grateful that we have an opportunity to make a difference in the life of someone we love. I don't think that list was supposed be an all or nothing proposition.

> The one absolutely unselfish friend
> that man can have in this selfish world,
> the one that never deserts him,
> the one that never proves ungrateful or treacherous,
> is his dog...
> He will kiss the hand that has no food to offer;
> he will lick the wounds and sores that come in encounters
> with the roughness of the world...

When all other friends desert, he remains.

—George G. Vest

If there was ever a living creature that exemplified the majority, if not all, of the attributes we look for when we think of unconditional love, the dog is it. The dog doesn't wait to see if it's loved first, it offers you love and then waits. Dogs seem to seek out those who need love instead of seeking out those who will love them. Rocky was (and is) the epitome of this trait.

It was easy to love Rocky, it was easy to take care of Rocky. In fact, he's the easiest of all the dogs we've ever cared for. The ease of it all lent itself to all of us holding a special place in our hearts for Rocky, and this was before we decided to adopt him. That special place was different for each one of us, we all saw a quality in Rocky and each of us saw something a little different. But everyone in the house saw the connection between Rocky and me. Elissa described him as a *healer*.

What Elissa, and Matt, and Corey saw was a dog who was in tune with me. They witnessed a dog who knew what other people were feeling, especially me. If I was having a good day with relatively little pain, Rocky ran and played with the other dogs. But if I was having a bad day, with significant pain, Rocky wouldn't leave my side. That remains the case to this day.

His most endearing behavior occurs when I'm lying down. If I'm having a bad day and need to lie down, Rocky follows me and lies down with me. There could be an all-out tug-of-war going on in the family room with Rocky enjoying the game, but if I get up from the living room and head upstairs, he immediately stops what he's doing and follows me up the stairs and jumps in bed waiting for me to get in. It's as if there is some invisible connection between us. If I'm okay, he's a regular dog without a care in the world; if I'm not doing okay, nothing else in the world matters to him.

That would be special enough—a dog that is so in tune with you that he stays by your side when you're not feeling well. But it's what he does next that gives Elissa reason to call him a healer.

When I lie in bed, Rocky gets himself next to me and positions his head in the area of my body that's hurting. If my lower back is hurting, Rocky's head will be there; if it's my leg, Rocky's head is next to my leg; if it's my foot, you guessed it, Rocky's head is there. Sometimes it's my neck or head, and that's where Rocky's head can be found. And then, as I'm lying there waiting for the medication that Elissa gives me to kick in, Rocky begins to gently lick the part of my body that's in pain.

At first I tried to push him away, I thought it was just a coincidence. But the more it happened, the more I recognized it as Rocky needing to do what he could (in his canine mind) to make me feel better. I'm lucky because Rocky's kisses—his licks—are soft and almost dry. My skin isn't covered with his slobber when he licks me, it's almost as dry as the rest of the skin on my body.

Do his kisses magically take away my pain? No, of course not. But what he does give me is a sense of comfort that medication can't come close to matching. He's so intent on helping me that if I have covers over me when I lie down, he'll burrow under them to get to the part of my body that's in pain. The best part of *Rocky Therapy* is that there are no side effects! Except an overwhelming feeling of love.

Rocky exhibited the same behavior when we had Shadow and Bear. He sensed they were sick and he would lie down next to them and lick the sores on their bodies as well as the growths. We'd watch him do this for hours on end and whatever growths he licked were the first ones to fall off each dog. Can you believe that? The growths that Rocky licked were the ones that fell off, and the sores that he licked were the ones that healed first.

What did Rocky know that no one else knew? How does he know when I'm in pain? And how does he know *where* the pain is? Instinctual? That's our best guess, and it's only a guess. All we can do is speculate. We'll never know the answers to these questions, but what is unquestionable is Rocky's desire to love.

You and I have desires. We have desires to love and be loved. Our hearts seem to swell when we're loved, our hearts beat faster and blood rushes throughout our body. That happens because of the way we're made to feel by another person. When we take responsibility to love another in a way that doesn't seek anything in return, we find ourselves heading toward unconditional love. When we seek to love more than to be loved, we not only make that person's day a little better, we make our lives a little better as well. You and me, and everyone else—we're all connected in a way that makes us interdependent on each other. When we practice the act of loving, we're generating a chain reaction of emotion. And that emotion leads to unlimited possibilities.

Think of where you work, where you live, your family, or an organization you're part of. Now imagine one act of love. Maybe it's being patient or kind, or trusting or hopeful, maybe it's even protecting. Whatever it is, imagine how the atmosphere around you would change with just that one act. What would it start? What do you have to lose?

Rocky, as a dog, demonstrates the best qualities we look for in a human. He loves more than he wants to be loved; he seeks to perform acts of love more than he seeks acts of love. Elissa and I sought to love him because of who he was, not because of how he made us feel. I'd like to think that he sought us for the same reason.

When we share love that is not self-seeking, that serves others instead of us, we not only make our day better, we make everyone's day better. Good News becomes great news for those we love as well as the ones who love us, even if we forget them and find them waiting for us in a flower bed.

Rocky lets Eiko take the lead in asking if he,
Reptar, and Dakota can go outside.

Rocky was the easiest (and calmest) dog we fostered; his
demeanor is just one of the reasons we fell in love with him.

Neiko

"What's in a name?"

When Shakespeare wrote this line in the late sixteenth century for his tragic heroine in the play *Romeo and Juliet*, do you think there's any way he could have known we'd be using this expression more than four hundred years later? One of the most quoted lines plays out countless times every day in our culture, now in the twenty-first century, a century of technology and a global economy. Sometimes the old becomes new, or at least it's recycled in a way that's purposeful in our lives.

Remember the first dog that I was responsible for myself, the one I had when I was nineteen years old? His name was Niko and he was a Siberian Husky-Shepherd mix. I loved Niko and he was not only the first dog I was responsible for, he was the first dog that I worked with to train him how to understand simple commands. We spent hours walking in straight lines along the perimeter of our small yard. I had him in a heel and my intent was twofold: to teach him the *heel* command, and to show him where our property line was. After this was established, we worked on *sit, stay,* and *down* commands. More hours of work paid dividends as he really seemed to enjoy the training sessions and our bond grew stronger every day we were together.

Remembering those commands would serve me well years later as a cop working a boring midwatch shift on a summer afternoon. We had a K9 unit working that day and I was very familiar with the handler and dog. The handler and I were friends and I frequently helped him train his partner, Blackjack. And by training I mean getting chewed up…again. This particular afternoon, Blackjack's handler needed me for a different reason, Blackjack got loose from him. He'd been let out in a local park by a creek and took off chasing some kind of wild animal. His handler, for obvious reasons, wanted to find him before any of the brass had to be notified.

He called me on the radio and calmly asked me to meet with him at an intersection close to the park. Police officers do this all the time; you've seen them—two police cars parked in opposite directions, right alongside each other. They're usually in a parking lot, off to the side. You're not alone in wondering what they're talking about. Most people think they're just wasting time. The truth is there are a lot of things that can't go out over the radio because anyone can pick up the transmissions with a scanner. A shift supervisor doesn't think anything of it when one unit asks another unit to meet at a certain location. And that's the way the two of us, Blackjack's handler and me, played it off that afternoon.

Our plan was to form a two-man perimeter in the direction Blackjack ran off. I took the side streets leading to the park and his handler went into the park. We were both on foot, calling his name. We were basically—literally—two cops looking for a lost dog in a park. Nothing special about that, right? Everyone in the department knew Blackjack reacted aggressively to the sound of handcuffs clicking, the sound they make when you're ratcheting them open to put on a bad guy's wrist. Most police canines react this way because this is the sound as a suspect is taken into custody. And the dog would love nothing more than for the bad guy to resist. I have to admit, it is a sight to behold.

So not only was I calling his name, I was also ratcheting my handcuffs up over my head in hopes the sound would draw him to me if he was close enough to hear it. Guess what? It worked! I was standing in the middle of the street with my hand over my head squeezing my handcuffs so they opened and closed, making that familiar sound that Blackjack knew all too well. We made eye contact about 150 feet from each other. As soon as he saw where the sound of the handcuffs was coming from, it was as if he had missile lock on me. He started sprinting toward me the way I'd seen him sprint toward me a number of times when I was training with him. Except those times I was wearing a *hit sleeve* on my arm, a thick canvas wrap that protects the agitator from having to get his arm sewn up after the training's complete. I realized this minor problem as he was closing in on me at full speed.

As far as what I was thinking and feeling at that moment, what was going through my head, I don't think I could give it justice by typing it out here for you to read. All I knew was I was about to be a chew toy for a highly trained police dog. Instinctively, I assume, I went back to that primitive brain that wants to survive and recalled the training I did with Niko. With Blackjack within striking range of me and still charging at me, I yelled, "Blackjack, no!" And then I screamed a command I'd heard his handler use many times, "Blackjack, out!" I repeated this once more and watched him hit the brakes and stand in front of me looking like he wasn't sure what to do. I think he was really confused whether he should chew me apart or listen to me. I'm grateful he went with the latter of the two. Once I had his attention, I commanded Blackjack to *sit* and *stay*. I contacted Blackjack's handler on the radio and asked him, nonchalantly, to meet with me on the street where his partner and I were standing (well, I was standing, his partner was sitting). The look on the handler's face when he pulled up was one of disbelief. He was certain that I would've been bitten and he was prepared to take me to the hospital if needed.

I asked his handler why he thought Blackjack listened to me. He replied because I used his name before giving him the commands. I learned that if you want to get a dog's attention, you first say his name. This is how they were taught in canine school and all of a police dog's commands start with the dog's name. What's in a name? Sometimes your life is riding on the line—especially if you're a canine officer and your partner is your only backup.

> May every sunrise bring you hope.
> May every sunset bring you peace.
>
> —Anonymous

Rocky and Eiko, if you recall, arrived together in our house, they were foster dogs from a shelter down south, and that shelter was going to euthanize them the day after we saved them. What a great feeling knowing we did something that saved another life! It doesn't matter if it's a human life or the life of a defenseless animal; if you can make a difference, you make a difference.

Rocky was the easygoing dog and Eiko was the wired Belgian Malinois/Akita mix who loved getting into trouble. The previous chapter was all about Rocky and how we failed at fostering by adopting him as our own. If adopting Rocky made us failures, keeping Eiko made us victims of failure. Taryn wanted to do something special for me. She wanted to help make a difference in the life of one of the members of the organization. She chose me. Taryn said that ever since she started the rescue, she wanted to donate a dog that would be used as a service animal that would make a person's life better.

When I discovered this act of generosity, I changed Eiko's name to Neiko. I simply added an N to the front of it. I changed his name because he reminded me so much of Niko, the first dog I had as a young adult. It was pronounced exactly the same, just spelled a little differently. I thought by changing his name there would be a stronger bond. Even though it wasn't a sixteenth-century play, Neiko changed his family loyalty and became mine. He became ours. After all, by assisting me, he would be assisting the entire family. I was grateful beyond words, I still am, for this gift that saved us tens of thousands of dollars.

Before I explain how Neiko became my service dog, you need to know a couple of things. The first is why I would need a service dog, how he could assist me, and why I'm in so much pain. So here's the back story on the pain and what's been hinted at in some of the pages up until now:

> In 2009 I began to have back and leg pain. I thought it was my sciatic nerve flaring up again. If you've ever had sciatic pain, you know what I'm talking about. And if you haven't

had sciatic pain, imagine a sword placed in a fire pit for an hour. Someone takes it out and then plugs into a wall socket so it's electrified. Now that person takes this red-hot, electrical sword and shoves it into your lower back so that the pain goes through your butt and down your leg. That's the kind of pain people with sciatica describe. But hey, I was a cop and a former martial arts instructor, teaching Aikido and Ju-Jitsu. I also taught defensive tactics and handcuffing techniques in police academies. I wasn't about to let a little thing like sciatica sideline me.

As the summer of 2009 turned into fall, Elissa didn't like the way I was walking and I began falling *up* stairs. That's right, I didn't fall down flights of stairs, I fell up the stairs. I also tripped over things on the ground or floor that I thought I had stepped over. After witnessing episodes of incontinence, Elissa told me I had to go to the doctor right after Thanksgiving. I agreed to go only to get a referral to see a chiropractor.

My family doctor and I have a relationship that goes back more than twenty-five years, I was one of his first patients when he joined a family practice in our town. My doctor listened to my symptoms and then did some nerve and reflex tests and said he didn't like what he saw. He was also concerned with the incontinence issues. He told me he'd compromise on my request to see a chiropractor if I got an MRI first.

The next day I experienced my first MRI. I was told that if I got nervous or felt claustrophobic all I had to do was squeeze the ball they put in my hand. The technicians slid me into that long tube and then the sounds started. That whirling sound was rhythmic and I fell asleep instead of being scared.

About an hour later I was putting my clothes back on and heading out the door. Before I left, the technician told me my doctor had written "*stat*" on the order so they were sending the results to him as soon as the films were read by the radiologist. I thought nothing of that statement and headed home. We had dinner and later I went up to the bedroom to watch TV while Elissa wrote lesson plans and graded papers.

Just before nine thirty that night the house phone rang. The caller ID was from my doctor, but he was calling from his home (the number was a local number from the hometown he lived in). How much good news does one get from their doctor when he calls you at that hour? He said he had the results of the MRI and I could tell by the tone of his voice that he was upset. The next words out of his mouth were, "Rusty, I don't know how to tell you this, but you have a tumor growing in your spinal cord."

Most of what he said after that didn't register in my brain. It was like Charlie Brown's teacher in the Peanut's series where all you hear is, "Wah wah woh wah wah."

But he did get through to me that I needed to see a neurosurgeon right away. He went so far as to reach out to a top-notch surgeon at the Hospital of the University of Pennsylvania earlier in the day, and I was told to call his scheduling secretary directly. I scribbled the name and number down and looked over at Elissa who stopped what she was doing as soon as she heard me ask, "I have *a what* in my spinal cord?"

I tried to explain to Elissa what my doctor told me. She had questions, lots of questions. I had confusion. And fear.

Elissa immediately went on the internet and searched everything she could about tumors in the spinal cord. We learned that tumors in the spinal cord are rare, *very* rare. They are so rare that there is no research being done on what causes them. They are so rare that they're considered *an orphan disease.*

I sat there, staring straight ahead for what seemed like hours. I didn't get much sleep that night, my mind ran through all the possible scenarios and outcomes of what this meant to me, and to my family.

I tried to hide this whole mess from my boss, but I knew I had to let him know what was going on. A cop who doesn't have his head screwed on right is no good to anyone. After reporting to the chief's office that morning, I learned that day would be the last time I would ever wear a police uniform.

I was able to retire, thankfully, with my full pension. I guess it pays to not use a lot of sick time or take all your vacation time every year. My retirement was uneventful as we concentrated on my health more than anything else.

I (or my MRI films) have been to neurosurgeons all over the country. From Philadelphia hospitals to a spine specialist in Miami, from a university in Texas to Johns Hopkins Hospital in Maryland, to the number one neurological center in New Jersey, and back to Philadelphia—we traveled everywhere to get a second opinion. Unfortunately all the second opinions were the same. The tumor in my spinal cord is considered inoperable and untreatable at this time. It's entangled in my spinal cord at the level of the third lumbar vertebrae (L3). If a surgeon were to try to remove it, I would probably be paralyzed by the operation alone. And unfortunately, according to my neurosurgeon at Jefferson Hospital for Neuroscience in Philadelphia, there is no way the entire tumor will ever be able to be removed. The most he'll be able to do is what's called a debulking, where he'll cut the worst part of it out and then put me back together and sew me back up.

If the tumor stays and continues to grow, it will paralyze me; the symptoms of that have already started. Some choice, huh?

The tumor has left me in severe pain that's controlled by both pain medication and modern technology. My neurosurgeon referred me to a pain management specialist who's been a true Godsend for me. You might have read about him a few chapters back, he's the guy who has patients willing to wait hours just to see him. His name is Dr. Kenneth Rogers.

I now have a *spinal cord stimulator* implanted in my back. The device is in the area just above by right butt cheek. Two wires run up along my spinal cord and they send electrical impulses into the nerves surrounding my spinal cord. This sensation basically confuses my brain so I interpret the pain signals as a vibration or slight electrical shock instead of excruciating pain. It works to the extent that it makes the pain bearable.

I also have what's called an *intrathecal pain pump* implanted. This device is implanted under the skin in my abdomen. A tube was tunneled around my side and up along my spinal cord, paralleling the wires from the stimulator. The tube end is secured in the fluid that surrounds my spinal cord. And that tube carries pain medication, pumped from the device in my abdomen, into that fluid.

Between these two devices, acupuncture, and a bunch of pain medication, I do okay. But I've been slowly losing my ability to walk without assistance and the feeling in my left leg is gone. I don't know where my feet are without looking at them, and I have what's called *foot drop*; the nerves leading to my foot are shot and I can't lift the front of my foot (my toes) when I walk. That's why I trip up the stairs, my toes get caught on the stair treads. And there are issues with incontinence and impotence. Other than that, I'm a regular athletic specimen!

So, how's your day goin'? It really doesn't do anyone any good to complain, does it? We all have *stuff* in our lives and when we look around, someone is worse off than us. So maybe it's best to be grateful for what we have instead of focusing on things that cause us pain.

And speaking of pain, you can now see why some people think I'm a real pain in the butt! But (not to be redundant), there are still things I can do and accomplish. And those things are made easier with a service dog named *Neiko* by my side.

> Dogs have given us their absolute all.
> We are the center of their universe.
> We are the focus of their love and faith and trust.
> They serve us in return for scraps.
> It is without a doubt the best deal man has ever made.
>
> —Roger Caras

Elissa and I worked like mad to try to get Neiko adopted. We blasted his face all over our Facebook pages, Corey and Matt did the same on their pages. People who were my Facebook friends checked my page regularly to see what antics Neiko had gotten into. I tried to share our journey with the foster dogs on my page and it helped share the individual personalities of each dog. Neiko definitely had his own personality and made for some great reading—according to everyone who commented on the pictures of the damage I shared.

There were days Elissa wanted to strangle him, and there were days he could do no wrong in her eyes. Me laughing at everything he did probably didn't help the situation, but he was so smart that I was often left shaking my head in amazement at what he got himself into. Like the time he opened up the bathroom vanity to get the 750-count box of Q-Tips out so he could play with them in the bedroom. Sure, I regretted that I showed him, once, how to open the drawers in the vanity, but if you can picture what 750 Q-Tips look like scattered across a bedroom floor. It was a picture you had to see to appreciate. So you can imagine my apprehension when Taryn told me that she was donating Neiko to me, to us. Boy was Elissa going to be surprised when she got home from work and I told her the news...

Having a smart dog who is easily bored can be both exciting and shocking. Now that Neiko was ours we knew we had to get him trained by an experienced person who knew how to train service dogs. We had to do it for him, and we had to do it for us—for our sanity and for the future of our marriage.

After three different local trainers agreed to help, but ended up not following through, Elissa and I found ourselves with a dog who was getting smarter and more bored with every passing day. I turned to the internet in hopes of locating a trainer anywhere in the continental United States. I was hoping somewhere along the I-95 corridor, but I would've taken just about anything by that point. What I learned was that there are a lot of unscrupulous people out there just waiting to take your money. These people prey on folks like me who are in need of a reputable dog trainer to train a dog for them. Fully trained service dogs, when purchased from a specialized trainer, can go upward of $20,000. Seeing-eye dogs are considerably more.

Elissa and I felt fortunate that we found a trainer in Jupiter, Florida, who specialized in service dog training and had more than forty years' experience training dogs. We made the two-day trip down I-95 with Neiko in the rear seat. We were excited and scared. We wanted Neiko to succeed and be the dog we believed he was meant to be. But we were scared too. We would have to leave him there for a minimum of one month before we would see him again.

When we arrived in front of a home that also serves as the business headquarters for Elite K-9 Academy, we knew things just got real. I tried not to let Neiko see the worry on my face, and I certainly didn't want him to pick up on my feeling of sadness that I wouldn't see him for a month. Any worries we might have had were quickly alleviated when we met the owner, Nick, who came outside to sit on his front porch and talk with us. That time also gave him a chance to evaluate Neiko. Nick said if a dog didn't have the right disposition, it wouldn't matter how smart it was. A dog that's going to be used as a service dog *must* have a gentle disposition.

After talking about our goals and Nick seeing how Neiko responded to simple commands, we went inside to his office and got to business. Inside we met his wife, Jeanneane, and she sat down with us and explained how the training process would progress. We had to write down our goals, read rules and a memorandum of understanding, and initial both. We were given more information than I thought I'd ever be able to absorb into my brain. That information contained basic obedience commands and their hand signals. We were expected to know these when we returned in four weeks. Finally, we signed a contract that included our goals and what Nick and his trainers promised to do.

Elissa and I were given a chance to say good-bye to Neiko before Nick put him in his kennel, a specially designed outbuilding in the backyard that houses no more than five dogs at a time. After we said good-bye to Neiko, Nick put him in his kennel and closed the door. Elissa and I could hear him crying all the way to our car. Leaving that house was the hardest thing I could remember doing in a long time.

Did Neiko think we left him? Did he think we abandoned him just like the dogs that had been abandoned at shelters that had come into our lives? We were heartbroken.

Our drive back to our *Snowbird* place in Jensen Beach took less than an hour. During that time all I could think about was how well Neiko behaved on our two-day drive down to Florida from New Jersey. We had to stop over in a motel and Neiko was better behaved than I expected, in fact he was like a different dog. All the anxiety of him acting like an idiot when we checked in was for naught as he sat next to me while Elissa completed the registration paperwork for our room. He was so well-behaved that when the duty manager heard he was being transported down to Florida for service dog training, she waived the $50 pet fee and wished us the best.

I was playing that over and over in my head. Was Neiko trying to tell us that he'd be a good boy and we didn't have to take him to a kennel for a month? Now I was having second thoughts and I was tempted to tell Elissa to turn the car around and go back to Nick's and get him. Our minds can really play havoc with our feelings, can't they? And let's be honest, guilt is a really strong emotion.

I didn't feel like eating, not lunch or dinner. Elissa knew I had to eat and made me a bowl of pasta. She was concerned my blood sugar would plummet if I didn't eat something. My cell phone rang while she was cooking dinner, I didn't recognize the number. It was Nick! His voice was cheerful and he seemed confused when I asked him what was wrong. Nick said he was calling to let me know that Neiko settled down shortly after we left and he had a friend in the program, his kennel mate, Chase. Chase was a Border Collie that Nick was training and he and Neiko hit it off immediately. Nick said he usually didn't allow two dogs to run in the yard at the same time until he was sure they would get along. But when he saw the way these two looked at each other through the wire that separated their cages, he thought he'd allow them to play. And boy did they play. Nick said they ran around so much that they were now exhausted, lying in their kennels. Nick thought I might want to know that Neiko was fine. He said he wanted to call me to alleviate any concern I might be having and to let me know I made the right decision. Elissa's pasta never tasted better.

> A dog is not a thing. A thing is replaceable.
> A dog is not.
> A thing doesn't have a heart.
> A dog's heart is bigger than any "thing"
> you can ever own.
>
> —Elizabeth Parker

Nick told me I could call him every night to check up on Neiko. I told him I didn't want to be a pest. He told me he understood what we were going through and if I didn't call to see how Neiko was doing in the days and weeks ahead he'd be concerned that we didn't care about him. I think we averaged one call every couple of days for the next month. And if Nick wasn't available to answer, he'd call back as soon as he could.

Finally the Saturday came when we would get to see Neiko; not just see him, I'd work with him on what he learned and the obedience commands we were told to have down pat. I felt like a little kid, I was nervous and excited and…and a little scared. This all got real; all of a sudden this all got real for me. I knew I was sick, but I never thought I'd be so sick as to need a service dog. I guess I got so caught up in the process of finding a trainer that I didn't realize the implications. I had an order from my doctor that stated I would benefit from the use of a service dog, and a statement from our vet, Dr. Cobb, that Neiko didn't show any signs of aggression. These two pieces of signed paperwork were required by Nick before he would sign the contract to train Neiko. All the paperwork, all the planning, all the worrying—and now it was all real to me. I really was that sick that the cane I was using wasn't giving me the support I needed. It was to the point that Elissa wouldn't go out unless someone was home with me. A service dog would not only give me more mobility and the freedom that goes with that, it would give Elissa freedom too. A service dog would give back to both of us a little bit of life that had been slowly taken away over the past four years.

We arrived at Nick's house to find trainers waiting for a group of us service dog handlers to show up. Each dog that was in the kennel had an owner—a handler—coming to work with them. This is the way it would be every Saturday for as long as it took Neiko and me to gel as a team and attain all the goals I listed when we first met. Each handler was assigned a trainer and I couldn't wait for my turn to go back in the kennel and get Neiko. Everyone out front was milling around and Elissa was introducing herself to the trainers, handlers, and the handler's families who came along. When Neiko heard Elissa's voice he started barking and howling. By the time I got to the kennel, he was going crazy. The trainer assigned to me stood next to me and watched.

Whenever Neiko met someone he would jump up and put his front paws on their shoulders. He would then proceed to kiss them until he was pushed away. He did this with everyone he met, including Elissa and me. I opened Neiko's kennel door and he immediately jumped up on me and started licking my face. He hadn't seen me in a month and he was as happy to see me as I was to see him. No sooner did he jump on me than the trainer yelled, "Off!" It was a sharp command with a tug on his leash to reinforce it. Neiko looked at him and went into a sit. The trainer explained to me that if I wanted to greet Neiko it would be by me getting down on my knees and saying hi to him calmly. I tried my best, but I was overcome by emotion that I hugged him around the neck as tight as I could. He got excited, let out a bark, and jumped on me again. And that got him another tug on his leash. Nick walked in and told me that Neiko was now a service dog in training, he was no longer a pet. Neiko had a purpose in life, he had a job to do and my job was to help him be the best service dog he could be.

It was tough love from Nick, but he was right. I had to put my needs aside and do what was best for Neiko. This was Neiko's life, he had a right to have his needs met more than mine. And right now he needed to show me everything he learned over the past month. We walked out to the front yard where everyone was waiting with their dogs. When Neiko saw Elissa he lunged at her and began crying. Now I had to correct him, I was holding the *smart end* of the leash. I gave a tug on the leash and yelled, "Off!" Neiko immediately got off her shoulders and sat. Elissa's eyes filled with tears.

Nick explained to Elissa what he told me, Neiko was now working, and when a service dog is working he must be 100 percent *on*, and that meant no distractions. Neiko was working with me and for me and we had to learn to gel as a team. Over the course of the next hour that's exactly what we did. At the end of the training session, Neiko went back into the kennel, but this time he walked right in and laid down. Chase, who also completed his session, went in next to him and also laid down. They had a system going and they were used to it. I didn't want to screw it up, so I told Neiko I'd see him next week and walked out.

Nick required all the handlers to spend at least Saturday's working their dog with a trainer. I asked Nick if we could come more often, and he told me we could come as often as we liked. For the next five weeks, at least three times a week, Elissa and I took the one-hour trip to see Neiko. I worked with him and Elissa worked with him. We worked on everything I asked Nick to teach him. We did public access training where we went to the international airport, the mall, restaurants, diners, and everywhere in between. We walked up flights of stairs together and down flights of stairs together. We worked on Neiko bracing for me when I was losing my balance and standing strong next to me when I fell.

Neiko was fitted with a special harness that has a rigid handle at the top, I use this for mobility support when we're walking and to help pull me off the ground if I fall. Of all the things we learned, Neiko's favorite was to brace. When he braced I was able to lay on top of him, completely on top of his shoulders if I needed to. When we were practicing this Neiko's ears went back and he leaned into me in a way that was both supportive and loving. He was in his glory leaning up against me knowing I was dependent on him for safety.

After more than two months of intense training, Neiko was ready to come home with us. It was conditional on the agreement that we continue to go to Nick's house at least three times a week until he believed Neiko had finished his training. We couldn't be happier and not only did Elissa and I look forward to the trip, Neiko couldn't wait to jump in the car knowing where we were heading. We cleaned up the things that needed to be cleaned up and tightened up a few things that I wanted to do. Neiko passed the Canine Good Citizenship test and we continued our public access work. Neiko ignored anyone and any animal around him. He paid attention to me and me alone when he was working—he loved *going to work*!

At home, Neiko wouldn't (and still doesn't) leave my side. Although he doesn't lick the painful parts of my body like Rocky, he absolutely knows when I'm in pain and he sits or lays at my side wherever I go. It's a bond that has gotten stronger every day. The time we spent together was unlike any other time I've spent with a dog. When I was in canine training with Boomer, we had to complete four hundred hours of scent work. We formed a bond that was noticeable by every member of the police department as well as my family. Boomer was my partner and we counted on each other to do the job of finding explosive devices. It was a bond that I still feel to this day. I couldn't compare that bond to anything else. I wouldn't try to compare the love we had for each other. It would be useless, so I won't. That was one bond. The bond I feel with Neiko is a different kind of bond. Neiko knows, somehow, that I need him in a way that no other dog can help me. He knows I'm dependent on him, he understands the situation, and he loves being a part of my life.

That kind of love is almost unexplainable. It's love based on giving of oneself for a cause greater than one's own. When we give unconditionally, we change the way the world was working before that moment in time. We set into motion a chain reaction that transforms reality to what it is—to what it should be. If we didn't act the way we did, everything following that moment of inaction is without our name on it. History, forever, will be that we did nothing and things went on in the same direction. If we do act, if we do give from the heart, history will forever be changed because of our desire to make a difference.

Neiko received so much in his training, and was now a service dog, because he gave so much. Elissa and I received so much in our training with Neiko because we were willing to put so much of our time and effort into it.

And me, what I received from a dog that we were willing to give up on is, quite simply, a gift. Neiko was a gift to me from Taryn, but I also see that he was a gift sent to me by forces I can't see or fully understand. He was dumped at a shelter at ten months old, he ended up at our home and almost destroyed it during the time he was there before he was trained. He came close to being given up on because his foster parents were too lazy to give him the time and energy he needed. It was pure luck that we found Elite K-9 Academy and Nick, who saw the potential in him. He excelled in his training, and he loves his work.

Neiko wouldn't be the dog he is if it wasn't for the idea of giving. At each and every step along the way, someone had to give in order for Neiko to move to the next phase of his life. Someone had to be willing to change history right then and there. Neiko received and continues to receive love, but it was through his giving of himself that he received everything. I received more than I ever could have imagined, at a time when I needed it the most. But I first had to be willing to give: I had to be willing to give Neiko a chance, I had to be willing to give the time needed to train him, I had to be willing to give into the diagnosis and prognosis that made me look at myself and give an honest opinion of what I saw, and I had to be willing to give a damn about life again.

In giving we really do receive. We receive more than we'll ever fully understand. When we give we change the course of history by setting a chain reaction in motion that will forever have our name stamped on it. Good News never traveled so fast.

Never teach a Belgian Malinois/Akita mix how to open the drawers in the bathroom vanity.

The author and Neiko learning to walk together during his training.

Boots and Socks

…It is in pardoning that we are pardoned…

Here is an email I sent to Elissa on a cold January morning a few years ago:

>I got up and put the dogs out; all went out except Neiko—who decided he wanted to stay in bed.
>I poured myself a cup of coffee and sat down.
>Then Bailey decided she had to go out back, so I got up and put her out.
>Next I refereed the playing in the family room.
>Took my first sip of coffee.
>Bailey barked at the back door, so I got up to let her in.
>The "Bailey Game" began as she ran away from the door each time I got up to let her in.
>I noticed that the dog's water bowl was empty, so I filled it.
>Took my second sip of coffee.
>Bailey finally decided she really wanted to come in, so in she came.
>When I let Bailey in, I noticed that Neiko left me a small lake in the kitchen.
>Got out the mop and went to town on that mess.
>Sat back down for my third sip of coffee.
>Watched Bailey puke up everything she had for breakfast (and then some) in the family room.
>Now the fun began—everyone thought it was their second feeding.
>Made a valiant effort to stop Boots and Socks from eating Bailey's puke.
>Realized my arm isn't long enough to reach from the family room to the kitchen sink to grab the paper towels.
>Dragged Neiko into the dining room.
>Pushed three dogs away from the puke.

>Ran to the kitchen to get the paper towels and the trash can.

>Dragged Dakota into the bathroom.

>Pushed two dogs away from the puke.

>Cleaned up puke with my hands while using my elbows to keep two dogs away from it.

>Proud of myself that I was able to multitask like that.

>Secured the trash bag filled with puke and put it outside.

>Went to the sink to wash my hands.

>Watched Neiko take a massive dump in the kitchen as I was washing my hands.

>Cleaned up Neiko's second 'gift' of the day.

>Washed my hands again.

>Took my fourth sip of coffee—it's ice cold.

>Put coffee in microwave.

>Sat back down to enjoy my coffee.

>Burnt my tongue because the coffee is so friggin hot.

>Now watching five dogs sleeping in the family room.

>I'm exhausted.

I sent this to Elissa at her work email to let her know how my day started. I tried to keep her in the loop before she retired. It kept current the connection she felt with all the foster dogs we had in the house. As you can see by the email I just shared, there were times we were taking care of *a lot* of dogs.

This was just one morning of one day that we were fostering dogs. It's not unusual for a foster home to go through this on a regular basis. If a rescue has twenty homes fostering dogs, it can get real messy. Collectively, that rescue organization can be generating a lot of waste on any given day. And not only do foster families have a lot of pee, poop, and puke to clean up, they have a lot of stories, both funny and heartwarming.

These funny and heartwarming stories were carried into the classroom by Elissa. Every morning she would write three P's on the board. At the start of each of her classes, the students were asked to guess how many of the P's Elissa had to clean up that morning before she arrived at school. The three P's represented

Pee, Poop, and *Puke.* The students who guessed closest to the actual number received a culinary treat.

The stories shared so far are just a sampling of what it was like at our home, affectionately renamed "The Williams Canine Hotel" by a few people on Facebook who were following the antics I posted on my page. Stories of puppies being puppies warm our hearts, we look at what they do with a sense of wonder and we tend to be more understanding when they get into trouble. We certainly wouldn't allow an adult dog to get away with the things we let puppies get away with.

Puppies chew on your stuff, you tell them to stop, your adult dog does it, you punish it like you're punishing your teenage daughter for not coming home on time. Puppies pee on the floor day after day, it's no big deal; your grown dog does it once, and you lose it. Puppies scratch you with their sharp nails, it's what puppies do; your older dog does it, you yell at it. Puppies jump all over people when they come over, you laugh and talk about puppy breath; your five-year-old Lab does it, and she gets yelled at.

Puppies sure do get away with a lot, don't they?

Is it because we look at dogs the way we look at children? We give smaller, younger children the benefit of the doubt, but older children should know better. That certainly is true of kids, but what about dogs? Do dogs have the ability to connect the dots and put all the pieces of the puzzle together to understand why they're being corrected? We treat them like they should be able to understand our human words and phrases, but the reality is dogs probably don't understand why they get yelled at so often, why they get their faces shoved in urine and feces, why they get thrown (literally) outside.

The research that I'm familiar with says you have about three seconds to connect a voice cue with an action by the dog. In other words, when a dog does something, you have no more than three seconds to acknowledge it for the dog to understand that what you're saying is connected to what they just did. This works for both positive reinforcement and corrections. If your dog does something that pleases you or completes a task she's learning to do, you have three seconds to praise her for that. That's the positive reinforcement part. Conversely, if your dog does something that's unacceptable, you have three seconds to get his attention and make a corrective action.

This means if you come home to a pile of poop on the kitchen floor, rubbing your dog's nose in it doesn't do anything other than make you look like a bully in your dog's eyes. Imagine if your child was at school and the teacher walked over to her and screamed at her, never told her what she should be doing (the expected behavior), and then walked away in disgust and didn't talk to her the rest of the class period. Would you be upset if your child came home and told you this happened? I bet you would. Especially if your child told you she had no idea why her teacher was so upset. Your child was doing her work like the rest of the class and the next thing she knew was that the teacher had an outburst and directed it at her. I know I'd be at the school the following morning.

This information I just shared is based on what I learned while working for Christine, the dog behavioral specialist, Nick, Neiko's trainer, and my ten weeks working with some of the best police canine trainers in the business when I was in explosive detection school with Boomer. I'm not suggesting anyone treat their dog a certain way, nor am I advocating any specific type of training or dog rearing. This is just a little bit of free information courtesy of yours truly. I strongly recommend you seek professional advice for any type of issues related to your dog.

Phew, that last stipulation should make my publisher's attorneys happy. If it doesn't, I am sorry for going out on a limb. I do seek your forgiveness as I apologize once again.

> There is no psychiatrist in the world
> like a puppy licking your face.
>
> —Ben Williams

When two little unnamed puppies arrived in our home one Sunday evening, Elissa and I were ready for just about anything.

We'd been through our share of dogs and nothing phased us anymore. Besides, puppies are cute and we were looking forward to a dose of cuteness in our house. These puppies were saved from a high-kill shelter and were part of a transport of fifteen total dogs that our organization took in on that transport. They looked like Lab mixes and couldn't be more than twelve weeks old. Their coats were pitch black, and each puppy had white coloring on their paws. The puppy with more white on his paws, the one with the white that went farther up his legs, was named *Boots*. The other puppy, the one with less white on his paws, was named *Socks*. Since they looked so much alike and were hard to tell apart, we came up with names that would help: the puppy with the least amount of white looked like he was wearing little socks on his feet, and the one with more white looked like he was wearing boots on his feet. Now their names helped not only identify them, but helped us keep them straight in our minds.

At the time they arrived, we had our Bailey, Rocky, and Neiko, and were still fostering Dakota. Two puppies should be able to keep this pack on their toes for a while, and maybe if they tired the pack out, Elissa and I would get some rest. Turns out that last expectation didn't pan out.

Boots and Socks had exactly the amount of energy you'd expect in three-month-old puppies. They not only tired the pack out, they tired us out as well! They were curious about everything. And I mean *everything*. We couldn't turn our backs for a minute without them getting into some kind of trouble. The more I thought about it, the more I thought we must have been nuts this time. The four dogs in our home were well-adjusted and we were basically on autopilot. There was a routine and everyone, humans and dogs, were on the same page. Now we made a decision that threw a wrench in to the process. What were we thinking?

Boots and Socks weren't the first puppies we had in the house that discovered the joy of a roll of toilet paper. I guess they saw it as a challenge—a full roll placed in a holder on the wall—to see how far down the hall they could take it without it tearing. If it was a contest, I can't say who won, all I saw was the aftermath: toilet paper strewn up and down the hallway, down the stairs, and back up into the bathroom. And every time I discovered the end result, I'd find them standing in the middle of the mess with their tails wagging as if to ask me if I was proud of them.

It would seem that if it takes x amount of energy to clean up after four dogs, the addition of two more dogs should increase that energy requirement by 50 percent. However, when those two additional dogs are puppies, and their names are Boots and Socks, the required amount of energy (and patience) is increased exponentially to a factor of eight! This was especially true of cleaning windows and doors—nose prints were the biggest culprit.

Our back door is a full-view glass door. The front storm door is also a full-view door. The windows in the living, family, and dining rooms all have low sills. Dogs of any size have no problem looking out of the aforementioned exterior wall openings. Boots and Socks, being the curious puppies they were, wanted to see everything — everything out the back door, everything out the front door, and everything out every window in the first floor. When two puppies look interested in something going on in the yard, it's only natural that the other dogs want to see what they're missing. First to join them at the door was usually Dakota, she wanted to make sure everything was safe out there. Next up was Bailey, who would bounce up and down excited to see anything different. Rocky would gradually make his way in between the bodies of dogs to ensure a sense of decorum. And of course, Neiko had to push his way in there to take charge of anything that might happen, such as barking. He took the lead in orchestrating that event in the house.

Six sets of nose prints, but not equally distributed, were on every window pane in the house. Our bedroom widows on the second floor gave all the dogs a better vantage point to see the entire front yard and street. Visitations by a flock of geese that lived in a pond down the street was always a cause of celebration for the pack. I really think the geese waddled down to our front yard just to see how pissed off they could get every dog in the house.

And speaking of our bedroom, please allow me to take this opportunity to share with you an event that took place one morning I decided to sleep in. Elissa had gone to work and it was just me and the dogs in the house. I woke up groggy and was on my way to the bathroom. Granted, all of my senses weren't fully functioning, but I do recall a peculiar smell. And it was right at that time that my brain was connecting with my olfactory system that I stepped in it. In my bare feet.

Look, I don't know how to dance, not one step. At wedding receptions I'm the guy standing at the bar, off to the side watching everyone's moves on the dance floor. I can't dance one lick. But on that morning I perfected the Cha-cha, the Twist, and the Electric Slide—all without missing a beat!

At least I was near the bathroom where I was able to grab handfuls of toilet paper and clean the *mess* out from between *my* toes. And jump in the tub. Then get back out to clean the tub with bleach. And then get back in to take a shower. I cleaned the tub differently than Elissa does. One of the most frightening and upsetting sights I ever witnessed in my life (and remember, I was a cop for twenty-five years and a paramedic for four years before that) was when I walked in on Elissa cleaning the tub one Saturday morning. I walked in the bathroom, and the first thing that hit me was the smell of bleach. In Elissa's mind, if a little bleach is a good thing, a lot of bleach is a better thing. The bathtub walls and glass shower doors have had more bleach on them than an *I don't know what*. You can probably think of an analogy for this better than me.

But what you can't think of, or picture in your mind, is something as scary as what I walked in on that Saturday morning. I stepped into the bathroom to find Elissa standing in the tub, holding a bottle of spray bleach in one hand a scrub brush in the other, completely naked. *Com-plete-ly* naked. Completely naked except for wearing a pair of yellow Playtex dishwashing gloves. There was my bride, standing in the tub, naked, wearing a pair of bright yellow dishwashing gloves, and all she could muster was, "Hey, what's up?"

What's up? I'll tell you *what's up*: My fear level is up, that's what's up! What the hell is going on? Her response was one of indifference. She couldn't understand why I was so upset. She told me this was the way she's always cleaned the tub, this way she wouldn't ruin her clothes by getting bleach splashed on them. And then she went right back to scrubbing the tub walls.

Like I said, I've seen a lot of sick stuff in my life. But this one... this one hit me hard. Some things can't be unseen.

When there are a half-dozen dogs in your home, two of them puppies, there is usually an odor of bleach somewhere in the house. And, there is usually something that you wish you didn't see, something that can't be unseen. That includes things you wish guests in your house didn't have to see as well.

> The great pleasure of a dog is that you may make a fool of
> yourself with him and not only will he not scold you, but he
> will make a fool of himself too.
>
> —Samuel Butler

When a perspective adopter makes an appointment, you do everything you can to make a good first impression. If you have a wife, you usually stand out of the way and let her clean the entire house to make it look, and smell, like you don't have any dogs living in it at all. Even with six dogs living in the house, Elissa did everything she could to make it seem like our house—the interior—looked and smelled like it belonged in a magazine. If it did belong in a magazine, I would have suggested *Mad Magazine*...

It didn't matter how many dogs we had in the Williams Canine Hotel, Elissa believed the way the house looked was a reflection on the people living there so she did everything she could to make it look presentable. Floors were vacuumed, furniture was vacuumed, and floors were vacuumed again after the furniture was vacuumed. Air freshener was sprayed and candles were lit. God do we have a lot of candles. Not just a candle in every room; we have multiple candles in every room. And not one of them is the same scent. You want to talk about a synergy of smells? What doesn't smell like bleach in our house smells like potpourri!

We were told there was an approved application on Socks and they wanted to see him that afternoon. As had become our routine and game plan, Elissa would introduce herself and welcome the people into our home while I contained the rest of the pack outside in the backyard. Then, I would come into the house and introduce myself and share whatever information we had on the dog they were interested in. We'd answer any questions the people might have and make sure they felt comfortable for their initial meeting with the dog.

After I had the dogs settled out back, I came into the house and met the family that was interested in Socks. It was a mother and her two young daughters, maybe six and eight years old. Socks had run upstairs when this family arrived, presumably to bring them a toy to play with. Socks had a habit of hiding his toys under our bed and we assumed that's what he was doing while we got to know this mother and her children. They seemed nice enough, just not overly friendly. They didn't laugh at any of my jokes, that should have been an omen.

We called for Socks a few times during our conversation. The girls seemed eager to meet him. Elissa and I wondered what he was doing up there. Here we were, down at the foot of the stairs, and Socks didn't want to make his grand entrance. Finally, after we ran out of things to say, I called for him one last time. And just like that, he appeared. He rounded the corner of the hallway at the top of the stairs.

Picture, if you will, three adults and two children standing at the bottom of a staircase, all of them looking up to the top of the stairs. The landing at the top of the staircase was a blank slate, a clean palette for which would be painted a lasting picture for a mother and her two small children who wanted to see a creature they were hoping to connect with. Now envision this: a small black puppy appears, carrying in his mouth, a pair of my dirty underwear. That wasn't a typo, the editors allowed it to stay here in the book. Socks had gone into the hamper in the bathroom and pulled out a pair of my dirty underwear. It's unknown what his intentions were, we only knew that we had to find a way to explain this.

Elissa nearly peed herself laughing, I almost crapped my pants, and the two little girls were giggling like mad. Their mother, on the other hand, she didn't find this the least bit amusing. Seriously? If this wasn't the most ironic, un-choreographed comedic scene in the history of dog fostering, I don't know what was!

The more we laughed, the more upset this mother became. Thankfully Socks dropped them at the top of the stairs before he trotted down to meet everyone. He jumped up on the girls just like you'd expect a puppy to do. The girls squealed and got down on the floor to play with him. I tried to explain how curious Socks was about everything around him. I did this in hopes of explaining away this incident that obviously didn't sit well with the matriarch of this family. I'm pretty sure all the explaining in the world couldn't change her opinion of Socks. They left about five minutes after he came down the stairs, by far the shortest visit we ever had for a dog. And we never heard back from them.

Maybe it was for the best that this family had no interest in Socks. I can't imagine a dog thriving in a home without humor, without people in it laughing—laughing at things that happen in the world and laughing at themselves.

I'm happy to report that the next family who visited Socks fell in love with him immediately. Like the first family, they also had two small children. But unlike the first family, this one laughed at Socks' hijinks, and they were able to laugh at themselves. Elissa had tears in her eyes as she held Socks in her lap on the short fifteen-minute trip to their home a few nights after their visit. This family was inviting and we stayed with them for about an hour talking and laughing. When we left to head back home, Elissa once again had tears in her eyes. But this time they were tears of joy.

We were down to five dogs now and before we knew it, an application was in on Boots. This family we knew. Their children were older than the family who adopted Socks. Both their children went to the high school where I was assigned and Elissa taught. Their oldest daughter knew Matt and I knew the mother. This family had shown interest in Boots and everything to do with our rescue organization through Facebook comments. Evelyn sent me an email asking about Boots and wanted to know if she and her son, Connor, could stop over.

Evelyn and Connor came over the next day. Connor was still recuperating from a serious illness and he and I compared notes of where we were in our recovery. But me and my medical problems weren't the reason they came over; they came over to meet Boots. And Boots didn't disappoint. He ran right over to Connor, who was sitting on the couch, and jumped in his lap. Connor looked over at Evelyn and said, "Mom, look, he already loves me!" Well, that was all I needed to hear.

Evelyn and Connor stayed for about an hour, with Boots hanging around Connor more than anyone else in the house. Evelyn wanted to bring the rest of the family over before giving the final okay. So a few days later Evelyn and Connor came back with Evelyn's husband, Jason, and Connor's older sister, Erin. Once again, Boots gravitated toward Connor, but he had no problem making himself known to all the other members of Connor's family as well. Time seemed to fly by as we laughed and shared stories about our families. We found reasons to laugh. Connor and I had been through a lot and we still found reasons to laugh. In my mind, this was the family who deserved Boots, and I was sure they would show him love and affection in ways that he deserved as well.

The following evening we were on our way to their home with Boots, riding on Elissa's lap just as Socks had done weeks earlier. Our drive was less than half the time it took to drop off Socks, it was literally around the corner from our home. This time Elissa didn't have time to cry, we were there in less than five minutes. Boots' new family had the house waiting for him. He had everything a growing puppy could want at his fingertips, er, uh, paw tips.

Within two weeks we had said good-bye to two of the most ornery puppies that were ever in our home. Now we had to deal with the realization that instead of being glad they were out of our hair, they had adopted two families that would love them the way they deserved. Yeah, I said they adopted their families. Sometimes foster dogs adopt their families as often as families adopt foster dogs.

> Our dogs will love and admire the meanest of us, and feed
> our colossal vanity with
> their uncritical homage.

> —Agnes Repleir

Why were we sad to see two little troublemakers go? Why weren't we thrilled to be able to get back to our routine and be able to relax a little bit? Why didn't we rejoice that we'd finally be able to see out of our windows again? What was it that allowed us to laugh instead of get mad at them? Over and over again Boots and Socks gave us reason after reason to get mad at them, and all we can do now when we look back at it is laugh. Their nose prints had to be scrubbed off our windows and doors, and yet now we look back and smile.

Wonderful things happen when we let go of garbage and grab hold of gratitude. When we focus on pardoning others of their mistakes, we find our lives become lighter. We're no longer bogged down with all that stuff we've been lugging around. It's as if by forgiving others we've forgiven ourselves for making life harder than it was supposed to be. And let's face it, when you carry around a grudge, it weighs you down. Everything seems to revolve around the grudge, comments by others that are completely innocent in nature remind you of that person who you resent. Then your thoughts start to play games, and the next thing you know you're finding more reasons to hold on to that anger you had in the beginning.

When we forgive—pardon—we free ourselves from the burden of balancing the books and more often than not, we see our own lives needing pardoning. We become more in tune with those around us, and we become more aware of our words and the tone of our voice. And then we see the need to be forgiven by others.

Boots and Socks could have been remembered as pains in the butts, two puppies that created havoc in our lives and in the lives of the dogs who were already living in our home. If Elissa and I, as well as Matt and Corey, and their friends (shoes eaten, jackets peed on, snacks eaten) didn't forgive Boots and Socks for what they did, our lives would've never been as rich as they've become. We would have never met Socks' family and learned about their children. We would have never been able to learn more about Evelyn and Connor, their family, and the love they have for Boots, who they renamed *Hendry*. They love Hendry so much that they even set up an Instagram account and Facebook page for him.

I wouldn't have shared my stories with Connor, some very personal issues I was dealing with. And in return I wouldn't have been able to learn how to handle a few of the more embarrassing symptoms of my disease, pointers and suggestions Connor gave me because he'd been through them and came out just fine. I learned from someone that I saw as just a kid up until I spent a few hours with him and his mom. May I be forgiven for not seeing the face of God in him all the years I've known him.

If each year in a dog's life equals about seven of our years, that means with the six dogs we had in our home at the time, we had a house full of toddlers, teenagers, and adults! I'm not sure which is harder—trying to figure out how each age group sees the world or how a dog sees the world? One thing is certain, they both have a unique perspective on what's happening just on the other side of their front door. And as hard as it is explaining to a couple of puppies what they're looking at, it can be even harder to explain to a toddler, a teenager, and oftentimes, an adult.

Maybe every once in a while the best thing we can do is share in their sense of wonder. Instead of trying to figure out what they're seeing or trying to explain it all to them, maybe they just need to know that we're there with them. That we forgive them and our pardon is unconditional.

Maybe all they need is to know that we're looking out the door with them, and wondering. And in doing so, perhaps the mess they make—the nose prints they leave on the glass—won't seem like such a problem in our world. Like footprints in the sand, they leave a story behind.

Dirty underwear, ripped-up toilet paper, and nose prints can be reminders of our need to be forgiven more than anyone else we know. Funny isn't it? Good News sometimes hides itself where we least expect to find it. Don't ever accuse God of not having a sense of humor.

I was going to get out the Windex and grab a paper towel to start cleaning the nose prints off the front storm door. Instead, I think I'll leave them alone for a while.

Boots looks like he's wearing white boots on his paws.

The learning curve where puppies figure out
cats rule can be an interesting one.

Yep, they did that to our bedroom.

Socks with the author's underwear during
an important meet and greet.

You and Me

...And it is in dying that we are born
into Eternal Life.

Spoiler alert: This chapter *is not* about death and dying. At least not in the physical sense, not clinical death as defined as loss of pulse and spontaneous respiration. Although I have to admit, I was tempted to use this chapter as an opportunity to jump on my soap box and tell you my beliefs about salvation. But then I remembered a few chapters back where I promised no more preaching. And see, this proves my fingers weren't crossed.

The idea of dying is scary, though, isn't it? For most people the thought of dying is scarier than the idea of death itself. Dying is a process, death is final. And do you see what the writer of the Prayer of Saint Francis wrote in this next to the last line, the subtitle of this chapter? The writer used the word dying, not death. Dying is present tense, death is past tense. Why do you think the author of this prayer used the present tense form of the word?

I don't have a clue why the line doesn't read, "And it is in *death* that we are born into Eternal Life." But when you read it that way and compare it to the way it's written and has been said for almost one hundred years, you can see a definite contrast in meanings. Let's stick with the way it was written for the rest of this chapter.

This idea of dying *is* scary. The topic makes people feel uncomfortable. What if we can work our way past the fear of the topic and see it in a way that, while still uncomfortable, won't make us want to run away from the topic? Or close this book after you've read this far?

So many conditions of happiness are available;
more than enough for you to be happy right now.
You don't have to run into the future
in order to get more.

—Thich Nhat Hanh

We can't get to someplace else if we're not willing to leave where we are in the first place. You can't get there if you're not willing to leave here. It's a process to get *there*, wherever and whatever *there* is to you. If *there* is a place where you want to be once you learn and grow from life's events, then you have to be willing to let go of the old you. In essence, you have to be willing to let the old you (or part of the old you) die. In the dying of the old you, you're remade into the person you want to be. You've arrived at that place you had in mind when you made the decision to learn and grow. It's how we've all grown, how we've all gotten to this point in our lives. It's also how shelter dogs become foster dogs who become adopted dogs. And it's the process of how a house is transformed, over and over again, into a home.

The idea of everlasting life, if not a scary idea, is certainly a topic of strong opinions. But what if this isn't referring to perpetual life in whatever form of paradise we envision? What if, for the topic of this book, everlasting life meant something different from our idea of salvation? Our names can live on forever, the memory of our lives can, and should, go on for time eternal. They should be, in that context, everlasting. But it's not up to others to make that happen, as if they're responsible to maintain a collection of news clippings and photos of our time here on earth. That responsibility falls to you and me.

Our legacy, the history of our lives, is written by us; you and me, we're the authors of our legacy. What we do during our time here is what's going to be how we're remembered. The differences we make today in the life of another will have effects generations from now. We might be gone physically, but the impact of what we accomplished will remain undying. There's a saying, at least I think it's a saying (okay, I heard it somewhere), that goes, "You'll be remembered more for what you did than what you didn't do."

Our legacy is the sum total of everything we've accomplished in life, and I'm not talking about job titles, or wealth, or possessions. Our accomplishments must include how we helped others and how we made a difference in the life of someone who was in need. If not, it's just history. History refers to the past, to antiquity. Legacy refers to something handed down from the past; it has a deeper and more personal meaning.

The dogs that came into our home, from the first ones to the last one, taught everyone who came in contact with them something about the idea of a legacy. Each one of them was reborn. Again and again they were reborn into a new life. From the first families that had them to their time in a shelter. And then from the shelter to our home. And then finally from our home to their *fur-ever* home (as it's called in the animal rescue world). Their past died in order for each new beginning to take place. Their past died each time they grew, each time they moved from one place to the next, they left their past behind. When they arrived at their new place, they started over again. And even though for some it took a little time, they did it with tails wagging.

Situations that were unknown to them became familiar and they adjusted. And then they flourished. They left their mark on every heart they touched—from the shelter to our home to their new homes where they now run and play with owners who will love them forever. The legacy of each dog is being etched in time; day by day and minute by minute, they're creating their legacy by making life just a little better for everyone they meet.

You and I can do it too. Sure our tails won't be wagging, but we can go through life with a smile on our face. We can sow love instead of hate, we can forgive and instill faith in those whose life seems uncertain, we can offer hope by brightening someone's day. And we can do it all with a sense of joy that's contagious. We can seek out those who need comfort and understanding, and we can seek to love those who need it the most. We can give in a way that never seemed possible before, and we can allow ourselves to be forgiven. We really can do all these things, it's not like any of them are going to cost us anything. But we first have to be willing to be used as an instrument. And we need to be willing to die…

Once we understand the idea of what it truly means to be used as an instrument, to be a part of something greater than ourselves, our lives are opened up in incredible ways. Remember, it's not the physical dying we're talking about here, it's allowing the part of you that was holding you back to die off. In allowing that dying process to occur, we allow ourselves to learn and to grow.

Had Elissa and I not been willing to let go of what we knew to be stable and secure, like a house that wasn't turned upside down, we never would have learned all the lessons we learned by getting involved with a cause that was greater than our own needs. We never would have grown into the people we are right now. That part of our lives before we were crazy enough to say yes to this fun is still there as part of our history. We can't erase the past. But the selfish parts of us that didn't want dog hair all over the house, the self-seeking behaviors we had that gave security to the status quo, and the egos that made us believe it was all about us and our survival (even in the midst of a life-changing rare illness) have all died. And it was a process, it didn't happen overnight.

Like the physical process of dying, the changing of our hearts was a process that took time. And at times, it was painful and it felt like we were suffering. But we didn't give up, and it's not because we never had that thought in our heads. There was more than one time when either one of us told the other to call Taryn and tell her to come over and get a dog (or dogs) that was causing so much chaos that we felt like it was just too much.

Have you ever been there? Ever felt like it was just too much? Huh; looks like you're in good company again! This journey of mine has been anything but easy, especially the past five years. And this can't be stated strong enough: Elissa's journey, and Corey's journey, and Matt's journey have all been anything but easy since I was diagnosed on that cold December day back in 2009. Their lives have been changed dramatically without their consent; a wife who was married a little more than a year had her life turned upside down, and two children who were being taken care of by their father had to learn how to take care of him. Who could have blamed any one of them if they wished they could pick up a phone and call someone to come take this burden away from them? I'm sure there are times it's seemed like it was just too much for them. But they stuck with it, they didn't give up. Part of their legacy will be how they cared for their husband and their father. And I ain't the best patient (to put it mildly), so they should also be put in for sainthood!

If you ask me to be honest, I'm right there with you some days where I feel like it's just too much. It's not fair and I wish I could throw in the towel. Whenever I feel like that I think of those who are counting on me and those whom I count on. Two legs or four, there's a legacy to write, a story that needs to be etched every day, and every second of every day. What do you want your legacy to look like? What eternal word will be said about you? That word (or words) was never meant to be silenced. It just takes a spark and before we know it we're making a difference in the life of someone who needed help. A smile to a stranger, a compliment to a coworker, holding the door for someone who needs some extra time getting from one place to another, forgiving a loved one, asking your child for forgiveness, hugging your partner and saying those three words: I love you.

It's not going to be one big thing, or great project, that makes that chain reaction get going. It will be a little thing, a small thing, that's the first domino to fall. Small things done with big hearts, that's what's going to change things.

> When the world is so complicated, the simple gift of
> friendship is within all of our hands.
>
> —Maria Shriver

As an ordained minister I get called to do a fair share of funerals. They remind me of a poem that's become one of my favorites. It's titled "The Dash," and it was written by Linda Ellis shortly after her grandmother's death. In it, Ms. Ellis talks about the importance of "living our dash," the dash that's etched between our date of birth and the year of our death. I would suggest that we could do more than live our dash. I would like to think that we could turn that dash into an exclamation mark and really make a difference! Just like that punctuation mark right there.

Whether a dash or an exclamation mark, it's the time we're here that matters most. The time that we're here is a time for living. For the living of the new self and the dying of the old self. And in between there's learning and growth, there are opportunities and successes; there is even pee and poop, heartache and love.

So many of us are afraid we'll be remembered by our last worst action. We judge ourselves by our own worst actions. Our legacy, the everlasting part of our lives, doesn't have to be one of fear and judgment. We have all we need right now to make sure we write our legacy: it's our hearts. Our hearts allow us to go through periods of rebirth; like the trees that lose their leaves in the fall and regain them in the spring, like the caterpillar that goes into a cocoon to become a butterfly, and like the tide that falls in the morning and rises in the afternoon—we are remade over and over again because our hearts keep on beating as the change happens. And when we think with our hearts, beautiful things happen. *Forever* kind of things happen.

Maybe you and me, maybe we're like foster dogs and we just haven't realized it yet. There are times we find ourselves feeling like we've been discarded at some dark cold place. It could be that we feel like we're on a highway for hours and hours, seemingly going nowhere. Perhaps we're in a new situation where the surroundings are unfamiliar and we don't know a single person, or we might have just landed someplace where everyone seems to love us. Wherever we are on this journey, may I suggest *not* grabbing a pair of dirty underwear from a hamper and carrying it around in your mouth...

When we find ourselves thinking we've been dropped off at a shelter with the other discarded misfits of life, it might do us good to remember that it's temporary. No, you're not going to be euthanized! There are people scrambling to get a van down there or an airplane warmed up so you have a chance in life. There are people that you've never met, right now, plotting to bring you to safety. Even if it's a temporary foster home, you'll fit right in and thrive there until you find your forever place—the legacy that you'll write.

If you don't feel like you're a shelter dog right now, go out and find one! Seek out a shelter and help someone who feels like they've been discarded like a bag of trash. So many people are hurting and could really use your help. Maybe it's an elderly neighbor, or a friend you haven't spoken to in a while. Go visit your neighbor, call a friend. Your neighbor and your friend deserve better than to believe no one cares.

Just be careful. Like fostering dogs, it can become addictive. And before you know it, you find yourself doing it over and over again, making small differences in a big way.

Does anyone think the song, *What a Wonderful World,* could have been made famous by anyone other than Louis Armstrong? Did you just catch yourself singing the lyrics in your head? Me too!

What did Louis Armstrong see that we don't see? What did he hear that we don't hear? What stops us from thinking that this really is a wonderful world? I don't know about you but I don't want my legacy to be a cynical guy who only thought about himself. The legacy that I want to leave is how I live my life *today.* The thought of our legacy isn't about a future history book that has yet to be written, our legacy should be written today, by us. It *needs* to be written by us today. And every day.

Perhaps in the days and weeks ahead we can think about how we're etching that exclamation mark, the time we're here on this earth. And we can use that time to consider what we need to let go of, what we need to let die so that we might get to that place where we belong. In doing so we're not just making history, we're becoming the author of our legacy.

The last bit of Good News in this little book you're holding is a reminder that we were made to be born not just once, but over and over and over again. We experience a rebirth countless times in our lives. Sometimes there is pee and poop, and even heartache, in that process, but it always leads to love.

The author finds a place in bed to lay his head.

The author's wife, Elissa, is smothered with puppy love.

Elissa's nap includes (clockwise from the bottom)
Bailey, Dakota, Neiko, and Rocky.

Amen

The author, Bob Perks, tells a story about heartache and love, about life itself:

It's an encounter he witnessed of a man saying good-bye to his daughter in an airport terminal. Bob sees an emotional good-bye and hears each of them say to the other, "I wish you enough."

When the daughter went through the security check point to her gate, her father was left watching her walk away. Bob saw that this man was upset and asked him if he was okay. The older man replied that he just said good-bye to his daughter for the last time. When asked why it's the last time, the man told Bob that he's old and his daughter lives far away. He continued that he had challenges ahead and the next trip back for his daughter would be for his funeral. Bob asked the meaning of them saying to each other, "I wish you enough."

The man replied that that wish had been handed down from other generations; his parents used to tell it to everyone. He continued, "When we said, 'I wish you enough,' we were wanting the other person to have a life filled with just enough good things to sustain them." He then shared the following with Bob:

I wish you enough sun to keep your attitude bright.
I wish you enough rain to appreciate the sun more.
I wish you enough happiness to keep your spirit alive.
I wish you enough pain so that the smallest joys in life appear much bigger.
I wish you enough gain to satisfy your wanting.

I wish you enough loss to appreciate all that you
possess.
I wish you enough "Hello's" to get you through the
final "Good-bye."

(Used with permission, Bob Perks, "I Wish You Enough"
©2001)

This is a *good-bye* from me, at least for now. There are plenty
of more stories I could share, just no more room to fit them in the
book. Isn't that like life? We want to cram more stories into it, but it
seems like there's no more room. We certainly have more stories to
tell, more life to share. It's just that in order to start a new chapter,
we need to close this one up and start anew.

I would imagine most of us are familiar with the word *Amen*.
It's generally used at the end of a prayer, or as an interjection when
someone strongly agrees with what's being said, as in, "Amen to
that!" The end of the Prayer of Saint Francis, and the end of this
book, concludes with that one-word line: Amen.

When said, out loud or to oneself, at the end of a prayer, it usually
means a conclusion by way of affirmation of what's been said. It's
like saying, "I approve of everything that's just been shared." Or
in the case of most prayers, what's been asked for. May I humbly
ask that you join me in striving for more love and less hate, more
pardon and less injury, more faith and less doubt, more hope and
less despair, more light and less darkness, more joy and less sadness?
Will you join me in seeking to console others more than seeking
to be consoled, to understand others more than seeking to be
understood, to love others more than seeking to be loved? And to
realize how much we receive when we give, and how much we're
pardoned when we pardon others?

When we see the world through the eyes of a dog, even a
dog that's been discarded and given a death sentence—*especially*
through the eyes of a dog that's been discarded and given a death
sentence—we begin to understand things in a way that not only
opens our eyes, but that opens our hearts as well. Nothing shared

in any of the pages that preceded this one have asked, or even suggested, that you open your wallet to do anything special. This idea of making a difference in the life of another costs us nothing out of our pockets. And yet, it has the potential to make us feel richer than we ever dreamed possible.

An affirmation of any request or incentive can be powerful. It reminds us of the power we have, that *potential energy* that's inside each one of us, energy just waiting to be used. It's the kind of energy in a puppy's tail before it starts to wag. It's stored up and ready to go, and once it gets going, it's very difficult to stop. And it's powerful! If you've ever been hit by the wagging tail of a Labrador retriever, you know the force that's in that tail. And if you're a guy like me who's been nailed by that tail, in that area of a guy's body that's very sensitive, you know *exactly* what I'm talking about!

Power can be like that, can't it? It can be used in ways that cause joy and in ways that cause pain. When we affirm or strongly agree with one another that we want to share joy, that we seek to be a force of love, our lives are enhanced by simply helping another. By now it should be apparent that by thinking of others more than ourselves, *we* are helped in ways we might not have previously considered. Our lives are enhanced simply by enhancing the life of someone else.

Father James Keller is quoted, "A candle loses nothing by lighting another candle." His Holiness, The Dalai Lama, reportedly wrote, "Our prime purpose in life is to help others, and if you can't help them, at least don't hurt them." A guiding principle for physicians, *Primum Non Nocere*, Latin for "First do no harm," is a revered statement dating back to the nineteenth century (although it is commonly misconstrued to be part of the Hippocratic Oath). Take a look at them. They're phrases from various times in history and from very different social and religious foundations that all share a common theme.

They served as declarations for those who heard them. And they continue to be just as important today; you might even say they are eternally relevant, that the legacy of each statement is perpetual.

Simple phrases can do that, can't they? They can last forever in the memories of those who hear them. Things we never remember saying are stored in the hearts of people we know and love, and even in some we might not ever get the chance to meet.

So thank you. Thank you for spending some of your time with me. I know how precious time can be and I truly appreciate that you took time to share a little bit of my world with me. I wish you the best.

And, *I wish you enough.*

It's time to go now. I have to put the dogs out.

Neiko, Rocky, and Bailey wish you enough.

Acknowledgments

This book would not have been possible without the support, encouragement, and help – real, honest to goodness help – of so many people. This is my opportunity to recognize them.

While many writers place the Acknowledgments page at the beginning of their books, I asked my publisher to have it placed here in hopes you'll take the time to read it. Because I don't know about you, but when I read a book I tend to skip over the acknowledgments section and dig right in to the first chapter. Now that you've finished the last chapter, would you please take a few more minutes to learn about those who've made this book possible and join me as I share my gratitude?

First and foremost I need to express my gratitude to Mr. Ryan Tate and everyone at Tate Publishing for providing me a platform for my passion. I need to especially thank the following individuals:

Stacy Baker, Director of Book Acquisitions: You believed in me and took the time to read the rough, very rough, manuscript of this book; your kind words will always echo in my head.

Eden Pancho, my project manager: Your persistence kept this book on track and without your dedication to it, this idea of mine would never have gone from manuscript to finished book.

Wendell Azucenas, my editor: Thank you for working with me to make my thoughts sound – and look – intelligent (not an easy task!).

The members and supporters of Joe Joe's Place Animal Rescue: You are the energy that started all that is written in the pages here. All the foster families in this organization that save dogs in ways few can understand, you deserve the accolades. You've all experienced so much pee, poop, and heartache; but also, thankfully, love. To all of you who've volunteered and sacrificed so much, to those who've given so much of your time, "thank you," doesn't seem strong enough. Every one of you need to know that your work and your labors are your legacy.

Those who work with dogs every day, the trainers and dog behavioral specialists who devote so much time and energy helping dogs become all they're meant to be. I need to especially recognize Christine Nolan, dog behavior specialist and creator of Your Dog and You. Christine, your words and wisdom are always at the forefront of my thoughts and actions when it comes to working with dogs. Thank you for sharing your insights with me and my family.

Nick Kutsukos, owner of Elite K9 Academy: Nick, you taught me more about life than you'll ever know. You didn't just teach me about dogs, you taught me about life. Your knowledge in training service dogs is amazing. You and your staff pushed me and Elissa in ways we never imagined; we owe a debt of gratitude to each and every trainer on your staff. Most importantly, you and your wife, Jeanneane, cared for Neiko with love. And speaking of love, thank you for telling me to "go write a book." And to Jeanneane: Thank you for sharing your time and talents in the early stages of this book, but most importantly, thank you for your friendship. It is a gift that Elissa and I will always treasure.

Dr. Lori Cobb, Pathways to Wellness Veterinary Care: Lori, your devotion to your profession goes well beyond what you've been called to do. And I firmly believe you have answered a calling, a very special calling that very few would even consider. If they could talk, I'm certain Bailey, Rocky, Neiko, Bojangles, and Bellagio (as well as Bosco and Boomer) would ask me to convey their gratitude to you and your staff for taking care of them, and Elissa and me, all these years.

The members of the Spinal Cord Tumor Association, a community of caring spinal cord tumor survivors, their families, and caregivers: Your encouragement and support have helped me and my family in ways that make words seem inadequate. You've not only helped my family cope with the daily struggles of this disease, you've given us hope. My prayers are with each and every one of you.

Those thousand or so friends on social media. Some of you I've known most of my life, others for just a few years, and still more I haven't had the pleasure of meeting in person – my cyber friends from around the world: None of you fully understand the impact you've had by way of your comments and posts. But you need to know how much they've helped. You've given me a chance to share my life with you and for that I say, thank you.

My friends, family, and colleagues who've been there for me and my family: To try to name each one of you would be nearly impossible and I'd probably screw up and forget someone. But know that you are not nameless; instead, you are precious. You are a precious gift to us and you know who you are. If you're reading this and we've had a conversation, or you've been to our home, or we've been to your home, or maybe we've met for a cup of coffee; whatever and wherever it was, you made a difference in my life and in the life of my family. Know that your legacy includes a cherished friendship.

My brother and sister-in-law, Glenn and Nancy, and their children, Drew and Anthony: You remind me every day of the importance of family, and without your love and support neither this book nor my success in life would have been possible. You've been there for us when we needed you the most; you've been there when I've fallen down and each time you've helped me up, sometimes quite literally. My gratitude goes well beyond what words could convey. I hope I've held up my end of the bargain by giving you all a laugh or two to help ease the pressures of life.

My children, Matt and Corey: A father never really knows if he's doing it right. But if the end result of any test can be measured by its success, then I think I have reason to smile. You two have given me more than just a reason to smile; you've also given me a purpose in life. I've watched you grow into young men who have taken on a role that you could have never anticipated. You are responsible for this book being what it is. For without you two, I would have never found my passion and my voice to write down what was in my heart. Corey and Matt, my heart swells with pride whenever I talk about you. Thank you for allowing me to be your father.

My beautiful bride, Elissa – my caregiver, my soulmate, my lover, and my best friend: What a journey so far, huh?! I've managed to write 80,000 or so words in this book in hopes of conveying a message; how is it that you leave me speechless? Maybe it's because it would take another 80,000 words to accurately describe my love and gratitude for you. Since that's not possible, I hope I can capture those feelings and write them here. Through all the craziness that's caused so many ups and downs, you've been the one constant throughout. You've been my rock, and you are my angel. Elissa, this book was your idea; it was your brainchild. You convinced me that what I had to say was worth sharing. The title was born from your thoughts. You were the first proofreader; sitting with me as I typed chapter after chapter, you read them over and corrected my mistakes. You were the first editor; you helped me see what I was writing and you made it better. And you were the first to read this book; it was the smile on your face when you finished the last page that told me we created something beautiful. The fact is, you are the first one I think of when I open my eyes each morning, and the last I think of when I close my eyes at night. Without you, there is no book. From the bottom of my heart, and with all my love – thank you.

Finally, my mom and dad: I hope I've made you proud. It's been thirty years since I've heard your voices, since I've felt your touch. It's been three decades since I smelled your perfume, mom; it's been just as long since I noticed your aftershave, dad. That's a long time to miss someone. I still miss you both, every day. What I wouldn't give to hear your voices just one more time; what I wouldn't give to feel your touch, to be able to laugh with you again. Even for just a split second – what I wouldn't give to see you both, just one more time. It was you, mom, who taught me what compassion and empathy looked like. Dad, you shared your sense of humor in such a way that made me want to be just like you. And while I can't share this joy with you in person, I want everyone to know that you two are as responsible as anyone for this book being written, maybe more than anyone. I know I gave you both a fair share of pee, poop, and heartache. But look at how it ended – it ended with love. And for that, I am forever grateful.

listen|imagine|view|experience

AUDIO BOOK DOWNLOAD INCLUDED WITH THIS BOOK!

In your hands you hold a complete digital entertainment package. In addition to the paper version, you receive a free download of the audio version of this book. Simply use the code listed below when visiting our website. Once downloaded to your computer, you can listen to the book through your computer's speakers, burn it to an audio CD or save the file to your portable music device (such as Apple's popular iPod) and listen on the go!

How to get your free audio book digital download:

1. Visit www.tatepublishing.com and click on the e|LIVE logo on the home page.
2. Enter the following coupon code:
   abd6-9bbc-2c51-e3be-894a-2b70-d08e-e4fc
3. Download the audio book from your e|LIVE digital locker and begin enjoying your new digital entertainment package today!

CPSIA information can be obtained at www.ICGtesting.com
Printed in the USA
LVOW07s1609191015

458850LV00001B/231/P